CATHOLIC BIBLE
FOR CHILDREN

Illustrated by Tony Wolf

CATHOLIC BOOK PUBLISHING CORP.
New Jersey

NIHIL OBSTAT: Rev. Msgr. James M. Cafone, M.A., S.T.D.
    Censor Librorum

IMPRIMATUR: ✚ Most Rev. John J. Myers, J.C.D., D.D.
    Archbishop of Newark

(T-965)

Illustrations by Tony Wolf
Texts by Stelio Martelli

© 2007 Dami International srl, Milano-Firenze

English text © 2006 by Catholic Book Publishing Corp.
77 West End Road, Totowa, NJ 07512
All rights reserved. Printed in China.
ISBN 978-0-89942-997-7

Contents

Introduction

ALL throughout the pages of the Old Testament, we meet a God Who is so filled with love that He reaches out to His people again and again.

The first pages of the Old Testament tell us what happened at the beginning of the world. God created the world and all that is in it. He called Adam and Eve to live in His happiness, but they rebelled against Him. God then called a holy people through Abraham and Sarah.

He protected them against their enemies. He saved them from their slavery in Egypt through Moses. He made them a mighty nation with David as their king. And, most important of all, He made a holy covenant with them that He would always be their God and they would always be His people.

Even when His people turned away from Him, God did not stop loving them. He punished them so that they would turn from their sins and turn back to Him. He sent them prophets who taught them the ways of the Lord. He led them back from exile to the Promised Land.

The final pages of the Old Testament show that God's love is far beyond what we would expect. He promised His people that He would send a Chosen One to call them out of their slavery to sin. He prepared them for the day when He would send His only Son, Jesus, into our world.

Creation

IN the beginning, God created the heavens and the earth. The earth was totally lifeless, covered by a darkened sky. God said, "Let there be light," and He divided light from darkness, making the day and the night. He then divided the waters from the dry land, and there were seas and oceans, mountains and plains. He gave a command and plants and trees sprang up from the earth, and they produced flowers and fruit.

God then scattered the stars throughout the skies, and He placed them among the planets and the constellations. He created the moon to light up the night and the sun to light up the day. He commanded the waters and the land to be filled with every type of animal: birds, fish, snakes, and mammals.

He then said, "Let Us make humans in Our image and likeness, and they will be in charge of all the animals on the land and in the sea." And so God created the first man whom He named Adam. He showed His love for him by placing him in a wonderful garden in which there were four rivers flowing with waters that were clean and pure. The garden was full of lush pastures and fruit-giving trees. Among the trees in the Garden of Eden was one whose fruit Adam was forbidden to eat: that of the tree of the knowledge of good and evil.

God warned him, "You can eat anything you want, only don't touch the fruit of the tree of the knowledge of good and evil, otherwise you will die!" In this peaceful world where there were no enemies among the animals, Adam was all alone. God decided to give him a companion so that he would not be lonely anymore, and so He created a woman. God blessed them both and said to them, "Be fruitful and multiply and be masters of all the earth for I have placed in it all the things that you need to live."

Adam and Eve were innocent and lived happily, not needing anything, without any difficulties, not wanting for anything.

The Serpent

OF all the animals that God created, the serpent was the most clever and evil. One afternoon, in the heat of the day, it said to the woman, "Why don't you eat all of the fruit that is on the trees in Eden?" The woman answered, "We do eat them, except for the fruit of the tree that God ordered us not to touch lest we die."

"O no, it is not sure that you will die. In fact, you will become like God," the serpent cleverly hissed. The woman listened to it with great interest, and she went over to the tree of the knowledge of good and evil. She gazed at its fruit, and the fruit was luscious and smelled so good. She waited a bit, and then she grabbed one and ate it.

A little later Adam arrived, and she gave him one as well. As soon as he took his first swallow, the two of them looked at each other and they realized that they were naked and they became ashamed. They took some fig leaves and they hung them from belts around their waists to cover their nakedness.

They were confused and troubled when they heard the voice of God call them. Instead of calmly answering Him like they always did, they became frightened and they ran off and hid themselves. God continued to call out to them, and so Adam answered, "Here we are, Lord, we are in the bushes. We were afraid and ashamed because we were naked."

Thus God understood that the man and the woman had disobeyed Him, and He angrily called out, "A curse be upon you! Man, from now on you will toil in the fields, and you will only draw food from the earth with the sweat of your brow. Woman, you will suffer much pain when you have children. Remember man that you are dust, and unto dust you shall return!" Having said this, God expelled Adam and Eve from the Garden of Eden, and He placed two Angels with flaming swords at the gate to the garden to keep them out.

Cain and Abel

ADAM had named his companion Eve, a name which means "life." They were now living in a new world that did not have the peace and love of their old home. This was a punishment for their sin of disobedience against God. Adam and Eve had to work hard to eat. They made clothes for themselves from animal skins in order to protect themselves against the cold of the night and winter. They began to kill animals to protect themselves and also to eat. Eventually, though, a terrible day arrived in which even human blood was shed.

Adam and Eve had many children. The first two were boys. They were named Cain and Abel. Cain had a dark

spirit and he was a farmer, while Abel was gentle and he was a shepherd. One day Abel sacrificed the best lamb of his flock to God, and Cain made an offering as well. God, showing how much he appreciated Abel's generosity, looked upon his sacrifice and smiled. Cain felt ignored, and he became jealous. God asked him, "What is bothering you? If you do what is right, then all will be well. If you do something evil, you will have sinned." Cain let his anger and jealousy grow until it became hate.

One day he said to his brother, "Abel, let's go out into the fields." Abel followed him. They went far away from everyone else. Cain wickedly attacked and killed his brother. He then ran away, convinced that no one had seen what he had done. Yet, he quickly heard the voice of God: "Cain, where is your brother?" "I don't know. Am I my brother's keeper?" The Lord cried out, "What have you done? Abel's blood cries out from the earth. May you be cursed, and you will continuously seek refuge and wander the rest of your life."

15

Noah's Ark

THE descendants of Adam and Eve continued to multiply and spread out over all the earth. But it seemed as if the blood that Cain had spilled had fallen upon their heads, for as the years went by, they lacked respect and love for God more and more. God was now sorry that He had ever created human beings, and He planned to punish them severely.

There was only one person left with whom God was pleased. It was Noah. He was wise and good and just. He and his whole family always obeyed the will of God. God appeared to him saying, "I am going to send flood waters over the whole earth and they will wipe out everything that lives upon it. But you, Noah, you must build an ark. Make it strong and sturdy. You and your wife and your sons Shem, Ham, and Japheth and their wives are to climb into it. Then, you are to take two of each type of the animals that I created, a male and a female, so that they might be

saved with you. Take enough food aboard for you and the animals."

Noah got to work right away. He and his sons built the ark, following the instructions that God had given them. They had every type of animal get aboard: animals that walked, those that crawled, and even those that flew. Even though some of the animals were natural enemies, they all obediently climbed aboard, not resisting in any way. As they were doing this, the skies became more and more cloudy, and one could hear the rumbling of thunder. Just as the last animals got inside the ark, and Noah shut and sealed the door, the rains began to pour down.

End of the Flood

WHEN the rain began, people just thought that it was a storm. As the days went by, though, and the rain kept getting worse, they began to get worried. They asked, "What is happening?" It kept on raining. The rivers and the lakes broke over their banks, and people climbed up on their roofs to escape the waters. The water still kept getting higher and higher, and people fled to the hilltops, carrying their possessions and their flocks. When even the hilltops were under water, some of those alive climbed up the mountains.

The ark started to float away. The rain beat against it as the waters continued to rise. Everyone who was inside the ark realized that the anger of God was raging against the world. It rained for forty days. The water covered even the highest peaks of the mountains. Every living thing disappeared from the surface of the earth. There was only one big body of water, with all the people and animals buried under its waters. Not even the birds survived because they couldn't find a place to land and rest.

God remembered Noah, and He decided to stop the rain. He ordered the wind to begin to blow, and the wind opened up the sky between the clouds. One could now see blue skies here and there, and the rain grew lighter and then stopped completely. It took one hundred and forty days, however, for the waters to begin to recede, uncovering the highest peaks of the lifeless mountains.

The ark came to rest on a mountain called Ararat. Noah waited another forty days before he opened a window on the ark. He sent out a raven. It flew around, but it found that all the land

18

was still covered with water and it returned to the ark. Noah then sent out a dove, which returned to the ark exhausted because it had not found a resting place. Noah, discouraged, carried it back into the ark in his hands. Would dry land never appear again?

Noah waited another week, and he again sent out a dove to see what was happening. This time it returned, and it had a twig from an olive tree in its beak. Trees were finally emerging from the waters. The return of the dove and the beautiful rainbow glowing in the sky were sure signs that God's anger had finally calmed. They heard a voice that said, "Noah, come out of the ark, you, your sons, your wife, and your daughters-in-law, and all the animals. Each of you should go wherever you want, so that life might return to the earth."

Tower of Babel

NOAH'S sons, Shem, Ham and Japheth, were the founders of the various peoples who populated the earth. Each of them founded his own branch of humanity and they each guided them to their eventual homes. This is how they came to live all over the earth. These people began to be different from one another, but everyone still understood each other because there was only one language on the earth.

Eventually, all the descendants of Noah gathered together on the plain in the East that is called Shinar. They decided to build a city, and they wanted to construct a tower in the center of it. The tower was to be so high that it would reach to the heavens. God immediately understood that they didn't respect and love Him the way they should have. They were filled with pride and arrogance. God decided to prevent them from building their tower.

Instead of punishing men by killing them or destroying what they owned, the Lord only confused them. He gave each nation a different language that others could not understand. This meant that when the carpenter spoke to the bricklayer, he could not understand him. When the architect spoke to the workers, they could not understand him either. The workers, not being able to understand each other, could not keep up the pace. Soon they even abandoned their project. The city where that great tower was supposed to be built was called Babel. To this day we say that someone is babbling when we cannot understand what that person is saying.

People were frustrated because they could not do what they wanted to do. They even became foreigners to each other because we consider people who speak a different language to be foreign. Each group of people went its own way, going to live in different parts of the world.

20

Abraham

ONE of Noah's descendants, Abraham, went to live with another people in the land of Ur. One day, Abraham heard a voice call him from the heavens. He understood that it was God's voice, and he fell down on his knees. The Lord said to him, "Leave the land where you are now living, leave your home and that of your relations, and go to the land that I will show you. I will make your family into a great nation, and it will be blessed by all."

Abraham took his family and the families of some of his friends and after a long journey they reached the land of Canaan. The Lord appeared to him and said, "I am going to give your descendants this land." Abraham bowed down until his forehead touched the ground, and he built an altar there to honor God.

Abraham and his wife Sarah were both very old. But one day God appeared to them and said, "Abraham, I will bless you with the birth of a son. He will be the head of nations. Kings will be born from him." But Abraham muttered, "I am 100 years old, Lord, and my wife is 90 years old, how could I have a son?"

Still, the Lord had made His decision. In spite of how old they were, Abraham and Sarah had a son whom they named Isaac. He grew up to be strong and handsome. Isaac was the joy of his parents, and they saw him as the hope of his people and the renewal of their youth.

God wanted to put Abraham's faith to the test. One night He appeared to him and said, "Abraham, Abraham, take

Isaac and go with him up a mountain. When you arrive there, kill him, sacrificing him to Me."

Abraham answered, "I will obey you, my Lord," even though he had to choke down his terrible grief. Early the next morning he woke up little Isaac and two of his servants. He traveled with them toward the mountain, carrying the wood they needed for the sacrifice on their two donkeys. On the third day they arrived at their destination.

Abraham, brokenhearted, obeyed God's command and he muttered to his servants, "Stay here. I and my son will go up the mountain and offer our sacrifice." He tied the wood onto his son's back, and he said to him, "You take the wood, my son, and I will carry the fire and the knife." As they were walking along, Isaac said, "Father, we have the wood, the fire,

and the knife, but where is the lamb that we are going to sacrifice?"

Abraham answered him, "The Lord will provide the animal for our sacrifice." When they arrived at the spot, Abraham arranged the wood and some stones. He then ordered his son to lie down upon it. Isaac, confused, obeyed him. His father tied him up and was ready to kill him, offering up his blood and his life to God.

Just then there was a voice from the heavens that said, "Do not harm your son, Abraham. Now I know that you love Me so much that you would even sacrifice your only son to Me. Go back home, and you will be blessed." Abraham looked up and saw a ram caught by its horns in a bush. Abraham went over and took the ram and offered it up as a sacrifice in place of his son.

Jacob and Esau

ISAAC grew up, following the law of God, and when he was forty years old he married a woman named Rebekah. When she was about to have her first child, she began to suffer from terrible pains, so she called upon the Lord. The Lord told her, "There are two sons in your womb and they are fighting each other because each represents a nation. They will be rivals when they are born, but the older will serve the younger." Rebekah was amazed because in those days the younger brother would always serve the older.

She had twins, but they were very different from each other. Esau had red hair, and he was hairy all over. Jacob was pale and much quieter. As they grew older, they became more and more different. Esau would go with his father out into the wildest places where they would hunt goats and wild pigs.

Jacob, who was more gentle, would sit in the shade of his tent. Isaac's favorite was Esau, while Rebekah's was Jacob.

Once, Esau came back from hunting, exhausted and hungry. Esau saw Jacob resting in the tent with a steaming plate in his hand. He asked, "What did you cook, my brother?"

Jacob answered, "A plate of lentils." Esau said, "Give them to me, I am starving to death."

Jacob muttered, "I'll give you them for your rights as the firstborn." Esau answered, "It's a deal. Give me the lentils." He ate them and was full. Maybe he thought that Jacob had been joking, but he had been serious. From then on Jacob considered himself to be the firstborn. In those days, the first-born had more rights than the other brothers. He received a special blessing

24

The trick was quickly discovered because Esau soon returned from the hunt saying, "Here is the game, my father." Confused, Isaac said, "But who are you?" Esau answered, "I am Esau, father." Isaac said, "Then who was the man who pretended to be you, because I blessed him?"

"It was Jacob, father," answered Esau, who now understood everything. "He has betrayed me once again." But now it was too late, because no one can take back a blessing. Isaac sadly said, "Esau, you are my firstborn, but now you have lost your rights as the firstborn. From now on you will have to serve your brother." Thus, everything came to pass just as the Lord had predicted to Rebekah.

from his father, inheriting all of his goods and his place of honor in society.

Over the years, Isaac never noticed that his sons did not get along, especially because he had lost his sight. Not being able to see, he once asked, "Where is my older son?" Jacob quickly approached him and said, "Here I am, my father."

Thinking he was speaking to Esau, Isaac said, "Bring me a little bit of the game that we used to hunt together. Then I will give you my blessing." This confused Jacob a bit, but Rebekah reassured him by saying, "Leave it to me." She dressed him up in some of Esau's clothes, and instead of bringing his blind father a wild goat, he brought him a kid goat from the flock. Isaac asked him to cook it, and then, satisfied, he gave Jacob his solemn blessing. He was still convinced that he was blessing his older son Esau.

Joseph

THESE two brothers thus disliked and even hated each other. Jacob, fearing for his life, left home. He went to live in Haran with an uncle. This uncle had a beautiful daughter named Rachel. Jacob fell in love with and married her. His life in Haran would have been perfect if he had not longed so for his father's homeland. Finally, when he could not stand it any longer, he set out for home.

When he arrived at the border, he was met by a messenger who told him, "Jacob, your brother Esau knows that you are coming back, and he is on his way here with 400 soldiers to kill you." Jacob realized that there was nothing that he could do against his violent brother Esau. He humbly went to meet him, bowing down to the earth before him and offering him half of his flock. Deeply moved, Esau hugged him and the brothers were finally at peace with one another.

The Lord had planned a tremendous future for Jacob. One night He appeared to him saying, "From now on you will be called Israel, a name that means 'God's prince.' I will give you the land I gave your father, and kings will arise from your descendants."

Jacob had twelve sons, and Rachel, his beloved, died after the twelfth was

born. Jacob loved Rachel's sons in a special way, and so he gave one of them, Joseph, a many-colored tunic to show him how much he loved him. This only aroused the jealousy of the other brothers. They said, "Why? Joseph is younger than we are, and he seems to be more important." The jealousy quickly developed into hate, and the brothers decided to punish Joseph.

One day they took hold of him and ripped off his tunic. They threw him into a dry well where he would die of hunger and thirst. When they finished this, they peacefully sat down to eat. They looked up and saw a caravan of merchants from Ishmael heading toward Egypt.

One of the brothers said, "What good is there in letting Joseph die in the well? Let's sell him to these merchants."

This is what they did. They sold Joseph as a slave. As he was carried away, the brothers dipped his tunic in blood which they carried to old Jacob saying, "Father, father, look! Our brother Joseph was attacked by a lion and torn apart."

This broke Jacob's heart. He covered his face with his hands and said, "Yes, this is my son's tunic." He began to cry.

Joseph in Egypt

THE Ishmaelite merchants carried Joseph down to Egypt. They sold him to Potiphar, the captain of Pharaoh's guard. At first he treated the young man kindly, but then, egged on by his wife, he had him thrown into prison. Joseph remained calm, however, for he trusted in God Who protected and inspired him. He even gave him the ability to interpret other prisoners' dreams.

One night the Pharaoh had a strange dream. He dreamt that he was on the banks of the Nile River. Seven fat and strong cows came out of it and began to eat their grass. After them seven thin and bony cows came out and ate the first cows. Another strange dream followed this first one: seven stalks of wheat sprang out of one stem. They were full and healthy. Seven other stalks sprang out after these, thin and dried up, and these later ones ate the first ones.

Pharaoh looked for someone who could interpret these dreams. He was told that there was a certain prisoner named Joseph who was able to interpret dreams, and he had him led before him. When Joseph heard about the dreams, he said, "Your dreams mean that after seven bountiful years there will be seven years of famine in Egypt. O Pharaoh, you should name a wise manager who can store up the extra food in the good years so that the people will not die from hunger."

Pharaoh answered, "You will be my manager!" Joseph got busy and during the good years he collected grain in the storehouses so that during the coming famine no one would die from hunger in Egypt.

There was also famine in other countries as well, including the country where Jacob lived. He said to his sons, "I heard that they have grain in Egypt. Go there and bring some back lest we starve to death." His sons set out and came before Pharaoh's manager.

They did not recognize that it was Joseph, the brother whom they had betrayed. He, however, recognized them. At first he treated them harshly, but later, after he had forced them to make another trip, and they spoke to him about Jacob, he could no longer hide who he was or hold in his feelings. He called out, "Is my father still alive? Brothers, don't you recognize me? I am Joseph."

They were terrified, afraid that he might want to get even, so the brothers didn't say a thing. But Joseph hugged them one by one saying, "Go to Canaan and tell my father to come to his son Joseph here in Egypt."

Moses

AFTER Joseph died, a new cruel Pharaoh took the throne in Egypt. He issued a command that no one dared disobey: When any Israelite boy was born, he was to be thrown into the Nile River.

One day a woman from the tribe of Levi, one of the tribes of Israel, gave birth to a son. She loved him so much that she hid him so he would not be killed. Then three months later, entrusting him to the mercy of God, she went down to the Nile River with her daughter. She covered a basket with pitch so that it would float and she placed her baby in it. She then lowered it into the water, telling her daughter, "I can't stand to stay here. Remain here awhile and watch over your brother."

Not too far away there was a spot where the water was deep and clear and calm. Pharaoh's daughter went down there with her handmaids. Seeing the basket floating among the reeds, she asked them, "What is in that basket?" The handmaids answered, "It's a baby," and she ran over to take a look. The princess was a good and merciful woman. Moved with pity, she said to herself, "It must be an Israelite baby."

The baby's sister, hearing this, came out from the reeds where she had been

30

hiding. She said, "Princess, would you want me to call one of the Israelite women to take care of this baby?"

Pharaoh's daughter said, "Do it." The girl ran to her mother and told her everything. The woman was overjoyed and she ran forward to take the child in her arms. The Princess, not knowing that she was speaking to the child's mother, said, "I will pay you to care for him." When he was a bit older, his mother took him to the palace and handed him over to the Princess. She named him Moses, a name that means, "I saved him from the water."

Moses grew up in Pharaoh's palace, being raised as if he were a prince. He was taught by the priests and the wise men, just as if he were being raised to lead his people one day.

Certainly, the kind princess who had found Moses could not have imagined that he would one day become a great leader, a fierce enemy of her own Egyptian people.

Moses grew up strong, well mannered, and intelligent. He was well trained in the use of arms and leadership. Yet, he hardly knew anything about the Israelites who were living as slaves in Egypt. He didn't concern himself with them until he found out that he himself was one of them.

When he found out that he was one of them, young Moses approached the Israelites and found his brother Aaron who told him all about Joseph and what had happened to his people since he had died.

But Moses had been raised by the Egyptians, saved from death by Pharaoh's daughter. He found it difficult to believe that the Egyptians would treat the Israelites that poorly. He decided to go down to the Israelites and see for himself whether everything that he had heard was true. One day he left the palace without telling anyone where he was going. Anxiously, he snuck down to the camp where the Israelites had to live and work.

First Stages
of the Exodus

WHEN he arrived there, Moses saw the Israelites were being forced to do hard labor. They were constantly being lashed by their Egyptian taskmasters. When one of the Egyptians began to beat up one of the Israelites, he found that he could not control himself any longer. He walked over to the Egyptian and killed him. Believing no one had seen him, he took the body and buried it. He then returned to the royal palace, filled with concern.

The next day he went out to visit the Israelites again. He saw another Israelite being beaten up, but this time it was an Israelite beating up another Israelite. Moses stood between them and asked, "Why are you beating up your brother?"

The man who was hitting the other man answered him, "Who made you judge between us? Are you going to kill me as you killed the Egyptian guard yesterday?"

This is how Moses found out that everyone knew about what he had done. Even Pharaoh had heard about it, and his soldiers were looking for him to put him under arrest.

Moses fled that instant, eventually finding himself resting against a well in the distant land of Midian. He sat there exhausted when he saw some young women approach the well to water their flocks. Some evil shepherds came up, though, and pushed them out of the way. Moses got up and helped the young women, and the shepherds fled. The young women gratefully told their father, a priest of Midian, what Moses had done for them. He entrusted his flock to Moses, and Moses eventually married one of the priest's daughters.

This is how Moses, who had been raised in a palace, ended up as a shepherd. But God had something else in mind for him.

One day, while with his sheep, Moses saw something incredible: a bush that

was on fire, but which was not being consumed. Overwhelmed, he went over to the bush. There he heard a voice saying, "Moses, Moses, do not draw near. Take off your sandals because this is holy ground. I am the God of your fathers, the God of Abraham and the God of Jacob." Moses, terrified, bent down to the ground.

The voice continued, "I have seen the suffering of My people. I am placing them in your care. Go back to Pharaoh and tell him that you wish to lead Israel out of Egypt." Moses asked, "What will I tell the Israelites who follow me when they ask me, 'Who sent you?'" "You will answer that the Lord sent you. Do not fear; they will follow you. If Pharaoh prevents you from leaving, I will send plagues down upon him until he has to let you go."

So Moses returned to Egypt. There, inspired by God, he spoke to the Israelites and they trusted him. He and his brother courageously went to Pharaoh and told him, "The Lord, the God of Israel, has sent me to tell you to let His people go."

Pharaoh answered, "I don't know any Lord who can order me about. As for you, get out, and don't go stirring up any trouble among your people." From that time on, Pharaoh ordered that the Israelites be watched more closely and that they be forced to work harder.

Plagues in Egypt

DAY by day, Pharaoh grew meaner toward the Israelites. He threatened them and gave them more and more work to do. He did everything he could to humiliate them. The Israelites, so beaten down, went to Moses and Aaron and asked them, "Why did you ask Pharaoh to let us go? Don't you see how badly he is treating us now?"

Moses called upon the Lord and He answered him, "Go to Pharaoh and tell him to let you go. If he refuses to do this, tell him that I will lift My hand against Egypt and he will suffer from ten terrible plagues."

Moses and Aaron said this to Pharaoh, but, backed up by his priests, Pharaoh sent them away. He was not afraid of what the Lord would do.

God therefore kept His word. The Nile, which is a great river that supplies water which the Egyptians drank and used to water their crops, turned into blood. There was nothing but blood for seven days, but Pharaoh would not change his mind.

The second plague was frogs. Millions of frogs came jumping out of the marshes, the rivers, and the ditches.

They were everywhere, spoiling everything. Pharaoh, upset by what he saw, promised to let the Israelites go. Yet, when the frogs disappeared, he took back his promise.

So there was one plague after another: mosquitoes, flies, and sick animals. The Egyptians were tormented by insects, they lost their flocks, and they were covered by painful, infected sores. But Pharaoh would not change his mind.

The seventh plague was hail. It destroyed the crops in every field. It fell everywhere in Egypt, except in Goshen were the Israelites lived. But Pharaoh's heart was hardened, and he would not change his mind. So there was an eighth plague: locusts. They swarmed into Egypt and destroyed and ate everything that the hail had not destroyed. When Pharaoh would not change his mind, there was a ninth plague: darkness. There were three terrible, terrifying days of darkness in Egypt. Still Pharaoh would not change his mind.

So Moses proclaimed that there would be a tenth plague, the most terrible of all. Every firstborn of the Egyptians would die. The Angel of death would go over the land, visiting

the houses of the Egyptians but not those of the Israelites. Moses ordered each Israelite to kill a lamb and to put a mark with its blood on their doors. They did this. That night, at midnight, when the deadly plague arrived, the firstborn of the Israelites were kept safe. But every Egyptian house was filled with tears. One could hear weeping all throughout the land.

Pharaoh could not take it anymore. That same night he summoned Moses and Aaron and told them, "Go! You are free to go, you and your people!"

The Exodus

AFTER 430 years of slavery, the people of Israel set off to travel on their long journey to freedom in the Promised Land. They marched along in a long column, guided by Moses and Aaron. The Israelites carried with them all that they could gather together: their robes, their carts, and their animals. Moses also brought along the bones of Joseph, for he had asked to be buried in his homeland before he died.

The Israelites did not know the paths in the desert. They could easily have gotten lost and died, but the Lord Himself guided them along. They were led along by a cloud during the day and by a column of fire at night.

In the meantime, Pharaoh and all the people began to regret having let the Israelites go free. The Egyptians said, "They used to do our work when they were slaves. Now who is going to do their work for us?"

Pharaoh cried out, "Let's force them to come back." He went out in his battle chariot, followed by 600 other chariots and the very best of his troops. They soon discovered the route that the

Israelites had taken and followed after them. Instead of passing through the Sinai where they would be able to leave Egypt on their way to Canaan, the Israelites had set out toward the Red Sea.

The Egyptians cried out, "The Israelites have taken the wrong path. They are trapped between the sea and the desert. They will have no place to flee!"

This was true, but Moses had guided his people along that particular path because that is where God had ordered them to go. The Israelites, seeing the sea ahead and the dust raised by the Egyptians behind, feared that there was no way out. They cried out, "Moses, Moses, why did you lead us here? Now we are going to die in the sea. Why didn't you leave us alone in Egypt?"

Moses knelt down and called upon the Lord. He answered him saying, "Tell your people to march right up to the sea. When you are on its shore, raise up your staff over the waters, Moses, and they will split apart, leaving a dry path on which you can walk."

Moses hesitated for a second, but then he heard the shouts of his people who were at the point of panicking. He cried out to them, "Don't be afraid, calm down! The Lord will not abandon you. He will save you one more time!"

Egyptians in the Red Sea

THE Israelites followed Moses' orders and marched out into the sea. As they did this, a great miracle occurred: the waters drew away and a dry pathway formed at the bottom of the sea. The people of Israel passed through the sea with their carts and their flocks. The water, held in place by the will of God, formed walls that were liquid and at the same time solid.

Pharaoh arrived just as this was happening. When he saw the Israelites getting away, he shouted out, "Follow them! Don't let them get away!" He went forward, followed by his horsemen and his other soldiers. They were all heavily armed, and they shouted out their battle cries, but they would not win this battle.

The Lord was going to protect His people and punish the Egyptians. He ordered the waters to return to their place. When the Egyptians saw this happening, they were terrified. The walls of water seemed to melt and fell back where they belonged. The Egyptians were in the middle of the sea, unable to escape. They were covered over by the waters and they drowned.

The Israelites who had finally reached the other side turned around and gazed upon the waters of the sea. They saw the bodies of the drowned Egyptians floating on its surface. They exclaimed, "Truly the Lord is with us, He has shown us His miracles, and He will never abandon His people." Moses gave thanks to God and then ordered, "March on!"

They followed him, but the desert road which lay in front of them was long and difficult. They soon used up the provisions that they had brought with them from Egypt. Losing heart, the people began to criticize Moses again saying, "He keeps telling us, 'Forward! Keep going,' but when will we get there? Wouldn't it have been better to stay as slaves in Egypt rather than to die of hunger and thirst in this desert?"

Moses told them, "Trust in God and He will help you," for the Lord had revealed that He would send His people food from the skies.

That same evening, a huge flock of quail descended upon the Israelite camp. They caught and cooked them, eating until they were full. The next morning, at dawn, they discovered a strange, dense frost covering their campground. The Israelites didn't know what it was, so they asked, "What is it?"

Moses assured them, "It is the bread that the Lord promised you. Take it and eat it."

So the Israelites continued on their journey to the Promised Land. In the desert of Rephidim, they could not even find a drop of water and their water skins were completely empty. The people began to moan and groan still one more time. But God told Moses to strike a rock with his staff, and fresh water came bubbling out, enough for everyone in the camp.

I am the Lord, your God. You shall not have other gods but Me.

You shall not take My name in vain.

You shall keep holy the Lord's day.

Honor your father and your mother.

You shall not kill.

You shall not commit adultery.

You shall not steal.

You shall not bear false witness.

You shall not covet your neighbor's goods.

You shall not covet your neighbor's wife.

Even while Moses was speaking with God and receiving His law, something very bad was happening in the Israelite camp. Growing tired of waiting for Moses, the Israelites came up to Aaron (who was in charge of them while Moses was gone) and they told him, "Moses is not going to come back. The God he

The Commandments

THREE months after the people of Israel had left Egypt, they entered the Sinai desert. They camped in front of a high mountain there. Moses climbed up that mountain by himself so that he could draw near to the Lord.

God said to him, "Have My people purify themselves and pray. Three days from now I will show them My power and give them My law."

This is what Moses ordered. On the third day, while the Israelites were praying, there was the roar of thunder and lightning lit up the skies. A column of blazing fire appeared on the mountain peak. Moses approached the mountain with a group of young men led by Joshua. When they reached it, he bravely trusted in God's promise and climbed it alone.

When Moses had been on the mountain for forty days and forty nights, God spoke with him in a forceful voice. He gave Moses His law, writing His ten commandments on two stone tablets. These are the commandments:

and asked Aaron, "What have you done? Why did you bring God's anger down upon us?"

Aaron tried to explain why he had done it, but Moses would not listen to him. He cried out, "Those who are for the Lord, come here!" The men of the tribe of Levi ran over to him, and he ordered them, "Arm yourselves and go out into the camp. Whoever worshiped the idol and offended God must pay with his life!"

They did this, killing those who worshiped the idol. This is how Moses calmed the anger of God. He climbed up Mount Sinai a third time and the Lord gave him two more tablets upon which were written the commandments. When Moses came back, he ordered that the tablets of the law be put in an ark made out of wood that had been covered with the finest gold. The ark was called the Ark of the Covenant.

told us about is nowhere to be seen. We need a god who can lead us on our way. Aaron, you have to give us another god."

Aaron was afraid of them, so he did what they told him to do. He had them gather all of the gold that the Egyptians had given them. He melted it and formed a calf out of it. The people surrounded their idol, dancing and singing and praying, bowing down in adoration before it.

While Moses was on his way down from the mountain, he heard singing. He asked Joshua, who had been waiting for him, "Who is shouting and singing like that?" He soon saw what was happening and, angered by what he saw, threw the two tablets of the law on the ground. He entered the camp

Crossing the Jordan

THE Israelites continued their long journey, at last stopping on the other side of the mountains that surround the desert of Paran. Ahead of them was Canaan, the land that God had promised to Israel. There, they again lost their faith in God, which angered Him. As punishment, the Israelites wandered in the desert for forty years. They did not dare try to cross over the mountains into Canaan. Many of them died as they wandered along. Even Aaron, the brother of Moses, died. Still, Moses remained faithful to God; he never lost his trust in Him.

One day God spoke to Moses from the top of a mountain. He said, "This is the Promised Land. Now that you have seen it, Moses, get ready to join your fathers. You have seen the Promised Land, but you will not enter it."

Moses answered, "Lord, choose someone who can lead and guide Your people."

God answered, "Take Joshua and lay your hands upon him."

He did this, and brave Joshua took charge of the people just as they were about to enter the Promised Land. It should have been a joyous event, but the Israelites were sad because Moses had died. Just before he died, he blessed all of the tribes of the people of Israel. He was buried in the land of Moab by God Himself.

God then said to Joshua, "Get ready to lead the people across the Jordan River. Once you are there, I will give you all the land that you walk upon. Be strong, Joshua, do not be afraid. I will never abandon you."

So Joshua ordered, "Gather up your weapons and get ready, because in three days we are going across that river!" Everyone was more than ready to obey. Some spies were sent in, and when they returned they reported that the people of the land of Canaan were terrified of the Israelites. Joshua and the people broke camp and marched to the edge of the Jordan. Joshua ordered the priests to carry the Ark of the Covenant into the middle of the river. Everyone marched forward. When the priests entered the river, the waters upstream stopped where they were while those downstream continued on their way. They all crossed over on either side of the priests and they climbed up the other bank.

Joshua did what the Lord had commanded. He ordered twelve men (one for each of the tribes of Israel) to collect rocks from the river bed. They brought them into the camp to remember the miracle of the waters that had stopped flowing. They built a monument to commemorate the place where the priests had carried the ark out of the river.

The Israelites set up their camp in the land of Gilgal. This was their first conquest in their new land (which had been theirs in the days of old). The first city lying in their path was the city of Jericho.

Joshua was preparing the people for battle when he looked up and saw a man standing there with a sword in his hand. He bravely challenged him, "Are you a friend or an enemy?"

He answered, "I am an Angel of the Lord. The land on which you placed these stones is sacred." So Joshua fell down to the earth and prayed.

43

Jericho

THE city of Jericho was surrounded by a high wall upon which stood a large number of armed guards who would act to turn back the Israelites. Joshua was worried because he realized that they would lose quite a few men if they tried to conquer the city. Still, if he wanted the people to continue to trust him, he would have to lead them to victory.

The Lord appeared to him and said, "Joshua, have all of your soldiers walk around the walls of Jericho for six days. On the seventh day, have each of the priests take a trumpet and walk in front of the Ark of the Covenant. They should walk around the walls seven times. On the seventh time around, have the priests sound their trumpets as loudly as they can, and order all the people to shout out as loudly as they can. You will see the walls of Jericho come tumbling down."

Joshua summoned his officers and priests and ordered them to do what the Lord had told them to do. The men of Jericho watched them from on top of the walls, not understanding what was going on. On the seventh day, they carried the gleaming ark around the city as the priests marched in front of it. They sounded their trumpets as they walked. They went around the city seven times. The men of Jericho asked, "What are they doing? This is a really strange way to fight a battle!"

All of a sudden, the trumpets grew louder and Joshua ordered the people, "Shout out! Everyone, shout out as loudly as you can!"

The people of Israel shouted out so loudly that it seemed as if the noise would reach up into the heavens. The strong walls of Jericho shook and began to crumble, throwing the soldiers down to the ground. The city was defenseless. The Israelite soldiers climbed over the shattered walls, entering the streets of the city. This is how Joshua miraculously conquered Jericho. Everyone in Canaan heard about this and they were all filled with anxiety and fear.

Samson

SOMETIME after Joshua's death, a young farmer named Gideon obeyed God and brought the Israelites victory over their enemies, the Midianites. He then guided the people of Israel for forty years. He was a just ruler, but when he died, the Israelites once again abandoned the ways of the Lord and met other disasters. They were tormented by a fierce nation: the Philistines.

One day, an Angel appeared to the husband of a woman who had not been able to have a baby and he announced to him, "You are going to have a baby. Do not let his hair be cut. He is going to free Israel from the power of the Philistines."

They had a baby whom they named Samson, and he grew strong, wild and free in spirit. When he grew up, he fell in love with a Philistine woman. His parents asked him, "Why are you going to marry a woman from among those who persecute us?" Samson, however, wouldn't listen to them, and he married her. Once, while he was traveling to be with her, he was attacked by a lion. Unafraid of it, he tore it to pieces, as if it had been a little goat.

But Samson's marriage to the Philistine woman only caused him grief and anger. To get even, Samson left her and he destroyed the fields of the Philistines in a most unusual way.

Samson captured three hundred foxes, and he tied a burning torch to their tails and then set them free in the Philistines' fields. The animals were terrified, and they ran all around in the fields, setting them on fire.

Furious and indignant, the Philistines demanded that the Israelites send them Samson or else they would come out in battle against them. Three thousand men from the tribe of Judah went out and captured Samson. They were about to hand him over to the Philistines when he broke free of the ropes they used on him. He picked up the old jawbone of a donkey and he used it to strike out at his enemies. He killed one thousand Philistines and the rest of them fled.

Samson answered, "If you were to tie me up with seven cords that had been woven together, then I would be as weak as everyone else."

So Delilah waited until he had fallen asleep and she tied him up with seven cords. She then woke him up suddenly by screaming, "Samson, the Philistines are attacking!"

In an instant, he was able to break the cords. Then, laughing, he said, "Oh no, Delilah, you need nine cords."

She tied him up again with nine cords, but again he broke out of them. He even freed himself when he told her that he would lose his strength if she were to nail his locks of hair to the ground. So the evil Delilah accused him, "You don't love me, because you are always lying to me."

Samson was proud of what he had done. He wandered from one place to another. One day he met an incredibly beautiful woman named Delilah, and he fell deeply in love with her. The leaders of the Philistines wanted to imprison Samson, and they knew how evil Delilah was, so they said to her, "If you let us know the secret of Samson's strength, then each of us will give you one thousand pieces of silver." Delilah promised that she would do it, and she began to question Samson about it. She said, "Samson, tell me, what is the source of your great strength? What is the secret?"

They were not afraid of him anymore. One day, eight thousand of the Philistine men and women gathered in a great banquet hall. Someone suggested, "Let's bring out Samson so we can have some fun at his expense." This is what they did. Chained, the blind giant was led up to the room where they had gathered. They made him perform tricks for their amusement, and he had to act like a clown while he was standing

Death of Samson

SAMSON said, "Don't cry. It's all right. I'll tell you the truth. My strength is in my hair, see. If someone were to cut my hair, I would be as weak as anyone else."

This time Delilah knew for certain that this was Samson's secret. One night he laid his head on her lap and fell asleep. She silently let in some Philistines who cut the giant's hair right to its roots.

Delilah then shouted out, "Samson, the Philistines are attacking!" Samson bounced up to his feet, ready to fight them, but without his hair he was weak. They put chains on him and threw him to the ground. Overjoyed, they cruelly put out his eyes and brought him in chains to their city, Gaza. There, they set him to work, pushing the wheel for grinding grain as if he were an animal, and they constantly made fun of him.

48

between two large columns. To mock him, they assigned a young boy to guard him. But they hadn't noticed that over time his hair had grown long again. Samson, on the other hand, felt the old strength return to his muscles.

Samson raised a prayer to his God and he then leaned over and said to the boy, "I am tired. Let me take a rest. I'll lean against the columns for some support."

The boy answered, "Go ahead." Samson said a silent prayer to God, and he then cried out, "May Samson die along with all the Philistines!" He grabbed hold of the columns and then pushed against them. They wobbled, and then they fell down. The palace crumbled, burying everyone under it, and they all died. Samson killed more people that day than he had ever killed before.

Ruth

NOT all of the stories found in the Bible deal with war, blood, and violence. Some of the Israelite stories are gentle and inspiring, like that of Ruth.

Ruth was the daughter-in-law of Naomi, a woman from Bethlehem. Naomi and her husband Elimelech and their two sons traveled to the land of Moab during a famine. There their two sons got married, and they all lived in peace for a number of years. Eventually, Elimelech died, and a little later their two sons also died.

The unfortunate Naomi realized she had to return to Bethlehem. She said to her two daughters-in-law, "I am returning to my homeland where I own a field and have some relatives. I am old, and someone is bound to feel sorry for me and help me. You are still young. I am sure you will find someone to marry you. I won't hold you back; it's best if you return to your families."

Grief stricken, one of the daughters-in-law went her way, but the other, a woman named Ruth, said to Naomi, "Wherever you go, I will go. Wherever you live, I will live. May the Lord curse me if I ever abandon you." So Naomi and Ruth traveled to the city of Bethlehem, arriving there around the time of the harvest. It was too late to plant Naomi's field, and they had nothing to eat, so Ruth said, "If you give me permission, I will go and gather the grain that had been left by the harvesters in Boaz's field. He is a relative of Elimelech, your husband."

Naomi said, "Go!" Ruth went for the grain. She was so good, so generous, so humble, so beautiful, that Boaz asked, "Who is that young woman?"

They told him, "It is Ruth, Naomi's daughter-in-law." Boaz went over to Ruth and said, "Young lady, please feel free to gather grain here. I will order my men not to harm you. Feel free to draw water at my fountain."

50

Ruth asked, "Why are you so good to me?" Boaz answered, "Because you were so good to Naomi, leaving your homeland to be with her."

So Ruth gathered the grain, and that evening she returned to Naomi with what she had collected. The next day she returned to Boaz's field. Boaz felt himself falling in love with her because she was so beautiful, modest, and gentle. He wanted to marry her, but there was another man who was a closer relative of Elimelech. That man had the right to marry Ruth and to buy Naomi's field. Boaz went with some of his friends to speak with him. He said, "Naomi wants to sell Elimelech's field. Do you want to buy it?"

He answered, "I will buy the field." Boaz added, "Yes, but you will also have to marry her daughter-in-law Ruth so that the family will not perish."

He then answered, "I don't want to do that. I already have a family and I have to think of them. I must say no."

Boaz, overjoyed, ran to Ruth and as soon as they could they got married. This was already a beautiful love story, but there was more. Boaz and Ruth had a son named Obed, and he became the father of Jesse. He was the father of David, the great king of Israel.

51

When Samuel saw Saul, he understood that God had sent him and he said, "Don't worry about the donkeys because you are going to be the king of Israel." A little later, the twelve tribes of Israel gathered together to choose their king. They said, "Let the king be chosen by lot." When they drew lots, Saul, the young man from the tribe of Benjamin, was chosen, just as Samuel had predicted.

Saul became the king during a dangerous time. The Ammonites had laid siege to the Israelite city of Jabesh. The people living there had sent for help. The Ammonites were known to be ferocious warriors. This is why no one in Israel came when Saul summoned them to take up their arms. The young king was frustrated, and so he had two oxen killed and cut up into twelve pieces, sending one to each of the

Saul

THE Lord chose Samuel, a wise man, to be the spiritual guide of his people. He was a judge of Israel for many years, and the Lord revealed the word of God to him. The Israelites, though, wanted to have a king, and so one day they told Samuel, "Choose a king for us to lead and govern us."

Samuel prayed about it, but he didn't know whom he should choose. Just then, a young, handsome man came knocking at his door. The young man was strong and tall.

He said, "You are a wise man and you know everything. Can you tell me where my father's lost donkeys are? I've been looking for them for a long time."

of the soldiers told him, "O Jonathan, you ate something; now you will be cursed by your father."

Jonathan answered him, "My father is wrong. If all of us would have eaten something as I did, we would have defeated the Philistines even more soundly."

This foolish command that not even his son obeyed showed how bad a king Saul had become.

As time went by, Saul became more and more proud. He did not follow the ways of the Lord. More than once he disobeyed Samuel whom God had sent to him to reveal God's will to him. Samuel firmly condemned him saying, "Watch out, Saul. You rejected God's word, and God no longer considers you to be the king of his people." As much as that bothered Saul, he continued to reign upon the throne of Israel.

tribes. He sent the message, "Whoever doesn't obey Saul's orders will end up like these oxen."

Everyone quickly assembled and they defeated the Ammonites as well as the Moabites and the Philistines. Saul's son, Jonathan, fought alongside of Saul.

During one battle against he Philistines, there was a terrible struggle. Saul, who had a bad temper, cried out, "Cursed be anyone who eats before we have completely wiped out the enemy." This was a really foolish thing to say, because the men became so weak from not eating that it was difficult for them to fight.

Now Jonathan had not heard what his father had said, and he found himself in a clearing in the woods. He saw a beehive lying on the ground, and he ate some of the honey. When he had finished eating it, his strength returned and his eyes lit up. But one

David

DAY by day, Saul became more dark and depressed. It was as if he were suffering from a serious illness. In the meantime, Samuel traveled to Bethlehem as God had commanded him, for it was there that he would find a man worthy to be anointed as the king of Israel. In Bethlehem, Samuel found a red-haired young boy. He was handsome and strong. He asked, "Who is that boy?"

A man named Jesse answered, "He is David, my son."

Samuel then knew what he had to do. He called the boy over and anointed him with holy oil, secretly proclaiming him to be the king of Israel. And so God's plan was fulfilled. A short time later, Saul wished to find someone who could play the lyre because its music would comfort him when he felt depressed and overwhelmed. David was quite good at playing the lyre, so he was brought to the royal court. He played for Saul. Saul felt better when he listened to the music, and sometimes he even broke into a smile. He loved David and took him under his protection.

But there was always another war to fight. The Philistines invaded Israel again, and this time they brought with them a great giant named Goliath. He wore iron armor and carried a huge spear. Goliath stood in front of the Israelites and cried out, "Why have you all gone to all this trouble? Let one of your men come out and fight me. If he wins, the Philistines will be your slaves. But if he loses, you will be our slaves."

No one was brave enough to go out and fight the giant. Day after day he shouted out his challenge.

Then, one day, David said to Saul, "I can't stand it that this Philistine animal keeps insulting the people of God. O king, I will go out to fight him."

"You?" asked the shocked king, "You're nothing but a boy!"

"No, I am God's soldier."

"At least put on some armor, David, or Goliath will tear you apart."

David put on the armor, but couldn't even move in it. He said, "O king, I want to go fight Goliath dressed as I am."

He grabbed five stones from the riverbed, and he confidently marched toward the camp of the Philistines, carrying only his staff and a sling.

Goliath saw him coming out, and as he marched out to meet him he cried out, "What do you want, boy?"

"I am going to fight you, because you have been insulting the people of God for far too long."

Goliath roared with laughter. "Is that so? It won't be too long before the dogs

and vultures are eating your carcass."
Grasping his huge spear, he came forward. David fearlessly waited for him. He prepared his sling and the rock went flying out, striking the giant between the eyes. He let out a groan and slumped to the earth. In an instant, David was standing over him. He drew out the giant's sword and then, as a stunned silence descended on those who were watching, he cut off his head.

David and Saul

DAVID thus entered the royal court as a hero. He became a good friend of Jonathan, the brave son of Saul. The Israelite women would shout, "Saul had killed his thousands, but David has killed his tens of thousands!"

Saul, who always had dark thoughts, became jealous of David. That jealousy grew so strong that one day, while David was playing the lyre to soothe his mood, he tried to kill him with a spear. David barely escaped from the blow, and from then on there were bad feelings between him and Saul.

It was a strange relationship. Saul apologized to David and asked him to come back to court. Next he asked Jonathan to kill David. Then he repented again, and he gave David his daughter as a wife, saying, "You will be my son-in-law." What he was actually hoping for, though, was that the young man would take an important role in the army, go out and fight against the Philistines and be killed in battle.

Eventually, David had to flee. He sought refuge in the desert with a few of his followers. They were constantly pursued by Saul.

One day, Saul went into a cave for a while. He did not realize that David was hidden in the back of the cave. David could have easily killed the king, but he thought to himself, "Let it not be said that I was an assassin in the sight of God." So he cut off the hem of Saul's robe, although Saul did not know what David was doing.

When the king eventually left the cave, David shouted out to him and showed him the piece of his robe that he had cut off. He asked, "O king, why are you persecuting me? Can't you see that I could

56

have killed you, but didn't?" Saul then went away.

These were trying days for the Israelite people. Samuel, who had grown old, died. Around that time, the Philistines returned to fight against Israel. The Israelites lost a great battle against them, and Saul and his sons were killed (including David's friend, Jonathan). It almost seemed as if the kingdom of Israel would vanish, but as Samuel had predicted, David took the throne and led the people to victory. He conquered the Philistines and the city of Jerusalem which he made the capital of Israel.

David was a wise, generous, and strong king. Occasionally, though, he made some terrible mistakes. Once, for example, he foolishly fell in love with Bathsheba, the wife of Uriah, a soldier.

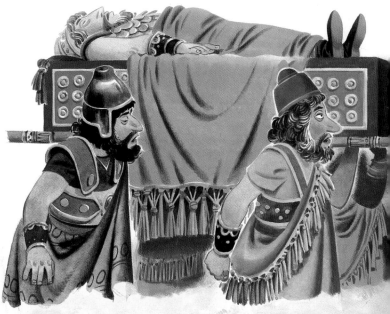

David wanted to marry her, so he had Uriah placed in the front line so that he would be killed. This is what happened, and the king married Bathsheba. This angered the Lord, and the next years were very difficult for David. There were wars, disappointments, and rebellions. Even Absalom, his son, led a rebellion against him.

Absalom eventually died, and David, who was growing older, was torn apart by grief. The only thing that lightened his spirit was his son Solomon who proved to be a good and wise man.

When David realized that his life was drawing to a close, he summoned Solomon and counseled him to walk in the ways of the Lord. The Israelites long mourned the death of this brave and successful king.

Solomon

SOLOMON then became the king of Israel. During his reign, the country became the most powerful it would ever be. No one dared attack them, for their borders were well protected. The king ruled firmly and wisely, assisted by many talented officials. His people were happy and successful. Israel was known all throughout the earth.

There is a famous story of just how wise Solomon was. One day two women came before the king with a newborn baby. One of them said, "O king, this woman and I live in the same house. We each gave birth to a baby three days apart. Yesterday, this woman's baby died, and now she wants my baby. Judge between us, O king."

The other woman cried out, "You're lying. My baby didn't die, yours died!" And the two women kept arguing with each other. So Solomon began to speak in a calm but severe voice. "Very well, each of you will have half of the baby."

He then ordered a soldier to cut the baby in half.

When she heard this and saw the soldier draw out his sword, the woman whose child had died said, "Do it!" The other woman, however, seeing that her child was about to die, cried out, "No, let him live. Give him to her, only don't kill him."

These words were filled with love and grief. Solomon therefore pronounced his judgment: "Give the baby to this woman; she is his mother."

Solomon decided to build a temple in Jerusalem, a house for the Lord. The temple would show everyone how powerful Israel had become. Thousands of stonecutters, carpenters, sculptors, and artists worked on this project in the heart of Jerusalem. The king searched for painters, goldsmiths, and other artists from all over the known world.

When he had finished, the temple proved to be one of the wonders of the ancient world. The interior of the building was covered with cedar from Lebanon. The altar was covered with the purest of gold. The king brought the Ark of the Covenant into the new building with a most solemn procession.

Two new royal palaces were also built in Jerusalem. Ambassadors came from distant lands, representing powerful kings who wanted to pay their homage to Solomon.

Solomon reigned for forty years, and when he died he was buried in Jerusalem. His son Rehoboam succeeded him, but he was not as wise or successful as Solomon had been. During his reign, ten of the twelve tribes of Israel rebelled against him. There were now two tribes left: Judah and Benjamin. Their kingdom was called Judah and their capital was Jerusalem, while the ten tribes were called Israel and their capital was first in Shechem and then later in Samaria. The king of Israel, Jeroboam, kept his subjects from traveling to Jerusalem. He renounced his faith in the true God and had his people pray before two golden statues of calves. Thus, part of Israel had returned to paganism.

Elijah

SOON, even the kings of Judah turned their backs on the true God and began to adore idols. The Lord then ignited a burning flame of the true faith in the heart of a wise man, a flame that would defeat Israel's infidelity. This man was Elijah. He feared nothing when it came to preaching the Word of God. He could even tell what would happen in the future. He gradually acquired a number of followers who were also called prophets.

The king of Israel in those days was Ahab, a difficult man, who married the evil Jezebel who worshiped the false god Baal. Elijah often bravely confronted them, eventually calling a long and terrible drought upon Israel. The people were hungry and thirsty. One day Elijah came before Ahab and challenged the four hundred and fifty priests of the Baal. He said, "Sacrifice a bull, and so will I. Place it upon a pile of wood, and so will I. We'll see if Baal is as powerful as the only true God."

This is what they did. Ahab's priests called out in vain for Baal to light up the wood. But as soon as Elijah called upon the Lord, a flame burst up from the wood on his altar. Then, when he prayed, rain began to fall to put an end to the drought.

will come down upon you and your family!"

Elijah never prophesied in vain. Sometime later Ahab fought against the Syrians, and he was struck by an arrow and died. Still later, the evil Jezebel was killed along with the sons of Ahab and all of the priests of Baal.

Elijah, however, did not die in his homeland. God had him travel to the other side of the Jordan. A fiery chariot came down from the heavens and carried the prophet up into the heavens in a whirlwind.

Even this was not enough for Ahab. He forced Elijah to flee to the desert. Ahab was more and more greedy, and he couldn't put up with anyone who would contradict him. Next door to his palace was a vineyard owned by a man named Naboth. Ahab told him, "Give me your vineyard and I'll give you an orchard." Naboth said, "It is an inheritance given to me by my father, and I won't give it to anyone."

Angry, Ahab spoke to Jezebel about this. She said, "Don't worry about it. I'll take care of Naboth."

Jezebel plotted against him. She had Naboth accused of blasphemy and stoned to death. She then boasted to Ahab, "The vineyard belongs to you."

Elijah then appeared before Ahab and angrily accused him, "O king, you are an assassin and a thief! God's anger

Job

THERE was a man named Job who lived in the land of Uz, and he was faithful to the Lord. He was very, very rich, so rich that his children could live a life of leisure. He was always careful, though, to make sure that they would never do anything that would offend God.

One day, Satan came before God and said to Him, "I have just come from the Earth." The Lord said to him, "Tell me, have you ever seen a man as honorable as Job?"

Satan answered back, "Job only honors You because he is rich. Take back his wealth, and see if he continues to honor You."

God let Satan put Job to the test, saying, "Do what you want with his riches, but don't touch him."

Satan set to work, and a messenger anxiously arrived and told Job, "Lord, some Sabean raiders came and stole your donkeys and cattle. Only I survived to tell you what happened." He had not even finished when another servant arrived to tell him that lightning had started a fire that had destroyed his stables, and it had killed his sheep and shepherds. A third servant came and told him that Chaldeans had come and robbed his camels and killed his servants. But the worst news he received was the last. He was told, "Lord, your sons and your daughters were eating and they were killed when the roof fell in and crushed them."

Job was overwhelmed by all the bad news, but he still said, "The Lord has given, and the Lord has taken away. Blessed be the name of the Lord."

In the heavens God said to Satan, "Do you see? In spite of his misfortunes and poverty, Job still blesses Me."

I was ever born, that I ever lived. I don't know why God is treating me this way, especially since I did not do anything wrong. Yes, God is just, but I am innocent. If He would only show Himself to me, I could prove it to Him. Oh, that He would have mercy on me, His servant, and let me die, or that He would send me some comfort."

This is when God intervened. He spoke from a whirlwind and He taught Job that he should acknowledge His greatness and accept His decisions without complaint. Yet, God now knew how faithful His servant Job was. Satan had certainly lost his bet.

God rewarded Job by restoring his joy. Job once again had children. Job praised God for His justice, and he lived a long and powerful life.

Satan answered, "Let me harm him and we will see if he still blesses You."

God answered, "You can harm him, but you are not to kill him."

Satan struck Job with a terrible illness. Job was covered with sores. He left his home and feeling miserable, sat down on an ash heap, far away from everyone else. Still, he said to his friends who had come to comfort him, "If we accept good things from God, should we not accept bad things?"

They had a long talk with him, but instead of consoling him, they accused him of having sinned. They said God must be punishing him for something.

Job patiently listened to them, and then he finally answered, expressing his sorrow as he said, "Woe is me that

63

waiting for hunger and thirst to make the people surrender. Just before this happened, a young and beautiful widow named Judith came before the counsel of the elders. She chided them for their lack of faith. She also asked for permission to leave the city. They gave her permission, but no one even asked her what she intended to do.

Judith dressed up in her most beautiful clothes, and she then went

Judith

THE great king Nebuchadnezzar ordered his general Holofernes to conquer Israel. Holofernes set off with a great army, and he arrived at the Israelite borders. The people of Israel had fortified their cities and fled to the mountains. Holofernes laid siege to the city of Bethulia, but he did not attack,

out to the enemy camp. The sentry there arrested her as a spy, and brought her to see Holofernes. The general was struck by the woman's beauty. She said to him, "O great warrior, I bring you a message from God. In a little while you will be coming into Bethulia."

Holofernes invited Judith to have supper and some drinks with him. He then ordered his soldiers to leave her alone. She was to have permission to enter and leave the camp at will. Holofernes fell in

64

love with the beautiful widow. He invited her to eat and drink with him again and again. Once, when he had too much to eat and drink, he fell asleep. What he didn't know was that this would be the last time he would fall asleep, for Judith cut off his head. She carried it into Bethulia and the next day the Assyrians saw Holofernes's head upon the city walls and they fled.

Jeremiah answered, "You have offended God, and His anger will come down upon you. Jerusalem will be taken. It and the temple will be destroyed. The Israelites will be exiles and scattered throughout the world."

The leaders of Israel put Jeremiah in prison and placed a yoke upon his shoulders. Still, he continued to warn the Israelites. The scroll on which he had written his prophecies was thrown into the fire, as if that were enough to turn back God's will for Jerusalem.

Jeremiah

Yet Nebuchadnezzar was still not through with Israel. He attacked the kingdom of Judah, threatening Jerusalem itself.

There was a man of God there, Jeremiah, who was a prophet. The king of Judah went to him and asked him, "What are we to do? Will God help us against the enemy? Will He save us? What is going to happen to Jerusalem?"

65

מנא מנא
תקל ופרסין

Daniel in the Lions' Den

WHEN Nebuchadnezzar died, his son Belshazzar, a strange and cruel man, became king.

One evening, during a magnificent banquet at which he had been drinking quite a bit, he ordered that the gold and silver cups that his father had stolen from the temple in Jerusalem be brought in. He explained, "I want everyone to drink from these cups!"

While everyone emptied their drinks, a hand appeared in front of the king and it wrote three words on the walls: *Mene, Tekel,* and *Peres.* There was a shocked silence. Finally, Belshazzar, disturbed by what had happened, ordered the wise men to explain the meaning of these mysterious words. But the wise men could not explain them.

The king, totally confused and pale, was unable to control his anxiety. The queen said to him, "Belshazzar, Daniel was able to explain your father's dream; now he might be able to explain the mystery behind these words."

The king called out, "Let Daniel be brought in." Daniel, a holy and wise young Israelite, came in. He broke the silence in the room by saying, "You have offended the Lord, drinking from these sacred vessels. *Mene* means that God has counted the days of your reign and they have come to an end. *Tekel* means that you have been placed upon God's scale and been found lacking. *Peres* means that your kingdom will be divided between the Medes and the Persians."

Belshazzar was very disturbed by all this, and he ordered that Daniel be given the honors of the third highest official in his kingdom. Yet, this did not save the king's life. That very night,

66

after the banquet was over, he was killed. The kingdom fell apart, just as Daniel had predicted. Shortly, Cyrus, the great king of Persia, conquered it and entrusted the province of Babylon to a prince of the Medes: Darius.

Darius left Daniel in his office. He was so impressed with his courage and wisdom that he considered putting him in charge of his entire kingdom. This made some of the other officials jealous, and they plotted Daniel's downfall. They said to Darius, "Lord, issue a decree that no one can ask for anything except from you. If anyone does not observe this decree, then let him be thrown into a lions' den."

Darius agreed with this, and he issued the decree. A little later, they told the king, "Lord, there is someone who is not obeying your decree."

He asked, "Who would dare to disobey me?"

They answered, "Daniel. We saw him praying and asking for something from his God and not from you. He must be condemned!"

Darius realized that he had fallen into a trap. He wanted to protect Daniel from a horrible death, but the law had to be obeyed. He ordered the guilty party to be brought before him.

He told Daniel, "I have to throw you into the lions' den. May your God protect you."

And so Daniel was thrown into the lions' den. Darius, upset, returned to his palace, but he couldn't fall asleep all night long. As soon as it was dawn, he ran to the lions' den and cried out, "Daniel, Daniel, are you still alive?" He heard an answer, "Yes. My God closed the mouths of the lions."

Awestruck, Darius looked into the lions' den. He saw that the animals had not harmed Daniel. He ordered that Daniel be set free, and that those who had accused Daniel be thrown into the lions' den. The lions immediately pounced upon them. This is how Daniel remained an honorable man.

Tobit

DIVIDED, with many in Israel not remaining faithful to their God, the kingdom suffered through dark and tragic times. Their last king Hoshea had been defeated and deported by Shalmaneser, the king of the Assyrians. Many Israelites were taken off into exile, and new peoples were settled in the Promised Land.

A large number of the Israelites who had been exiled ended up in the city of Nineveh. Among them was a religious man from the province of Galilee named Tobit. He was always faithful to God, and continuously performed works of mercy and charity. This was true even when he was in Nineveh, where he helped the poor, took care of the ill, and buried the dead.

But Tobit was about to face hard times. One night, while he was sleeping in the garden, some waste fell from a bird's nest and landed in his eyes, blinding him. Tobit, who could no longer see, could not work, so Anna, his wife, made a living for herself, her husband,

and her son Tobias by sewing clothing. Once she cruelly mocked Tobit saying, "What good did your being religious do for you?"

Around that time, Tobit remembered that a man named Gabael owed him some money. He said to Tobias, "Go, my son, and get the money back because we really need it."

Tobias set out, and he quickly met a handsome young man who offered to go with him and guide him to his destination. The two of them traveled together and arrived at the Tigris River. They jumped in the river to clean up a bit, and a large fish swam over to Tobias in a threatening manner. It frightened him, but his companion said, "Cut out the heart, liver, and gall bladder from the fish. You are going to need them later."

the gall on your father's eyes and you'll know why."

When they arrived home, Tobias did as his friend had counseled him. He rubbed the gall on his father's eyes, and at that instant, Tobit regained his sight. Tobias gave thanks to God, and he turned to his friend and asked him, "Who are you? How can I ever thank you for all that you've done?"

The young man smiled and answered, "I am the Angel Raphael, and God sent me because after He had tried you, He wanted you and your family to live in peace."

Having said that, the Angel disappeared from their sight.

They set out again, and after they received the money from Gabael, they continued on their journey. Tobias asked, "Friend, why did you tell me to save the fish's organs?" The young man answered, "When we reach home, rub

Rebuilding Jerusalem

INSPIRED by God, Cyrus, the great Persian king, issued a decree:

"The Lord of the heavens has given me all the kingdoms of the world. He has commanded me to build a house for Him in Judah, in Jerusalem. All those of you who belong to His people should go to Jerusalem and build a house there for the Lord. If you do not wish to go, then at least help the work by giving gold, silver, or whatever you can."

This was a great moment of salvation for the Israelites who had been exiled in Babylon. Many of them returned to their ancient homeland, carrying with them the ancient vessels that Nebuchadnezzar had taken from the temple in Jerusalem, the same vessels that Belshazzar had used on the night of his death.

But the kingdom of Judah no longer existed, and many different peoples were living there. Jerusalem was a devastated, ruined city. Yet, the Israelites only thought about rebuilding the temple so that it would be God's house and the spiritual center of all His people.

But it was not easy to rebuild the temple. Some wanted it to be just like the old temple; others wanted it to be totally new. Some people were sad; others rejoiced as they saw it rise up little by little. But everyone still continued to work.

Yet, the people's enemies remained. Some of the people in the city, others in the neighboring countries, and especially the Samaritans did not want the temple to be rebuilt. They knew that once the Israelites had finished rebuilding the temple, they would build walls

for the city and become rich and powerful again.

More than once, they interrupted the labor, and the Israelites had to place soldiers alongside of the workers. The project was difficult and exhausting, but the Israelites did not get discouraged. They carried on as God had commanded, remembering His words, "If you are unfaithful and arrogant, I will scatter you among the nations. But if you return to Me and observe My law and are faithful to My commands, then I will bring you back, even those who have been carried to the ends of the earth. I will bring you to My chosen land so that My name might live there."

Finally, a generous king was crowned and he issued a law that no one should dare interrupt the reconstruction of the project. The Israelites, rejoicing, redoubled their efforts, and the temple slowly took shape until it was completed. It was finally possible to celebrate the Passover again, and the dispersed children of Israel and Judah came to purify themselves. They were now one again, hoping for a new kingdom. The new temple was not as magnificent as that which the great Solomon had built. It did not have the riches that it once contained. Nevertheless, Israel finally had a house in which God could dwell.

It was God Who guided the Israelite people through the centuries. He had Moses free them from slavery in Egypt. He guided them safe and sound through the desert and the sea. He called Joshua through whom they conquered the Promised Land. He placed the kingdom into the hands of Saul, David, and Solomon, and He will continue to be with His people forever.

Introduction

THE New Testament is both a continuation of the story that we have already seen in the Old Testament and something very new.

In the Old Testament we saw how God called a people to Himself and how He made a covenant of love with that people. He promised that He would always be with them.

God never turns back on His promises, even when we turn away from Him with our sins. The New Testament is the story of how God defeated the power of sin through the life and death of His only Son.

Jesus was born, One like us, in a cave in Bethlehem. He went about proclaiming that the kingdom of God was near, and He called us to turn back to God with all our heart, soul, and strength. He called the Apostles and disciples to follow Him and to share in His mission. He gave us a new set of laws, the Beatitudes, which challenge us to be as loving and merciful and God is. And then on Calvary He took up His Cross and died for us, sealing His new promise, the new covenant, with His own blood.

Even then, His love knew no limit. God the Father raised Jesus from the dead so that death could no longer have power over Him and so that we could have the promise that one day we will rise with Jesus. He then sent His Holy Spirit to fill us with His life, making us into a Church.

Birth of Jesus

THIS is a true story about what happened in Israel over 2,000 years ago. The Israelites lived in that land, but it was ruled by the Romans who dominated most of the known world. The story begins on a starry night in the town of Bethlehem, the province of Judah. That night a carpenter named Joseph and his wife Mary arrived there because the Roman emperor wanted to know how many people lived in his empire.

Everyone was to go to the city in which they had been born and register with the Roman officials there. Joseph, who lived in Nazareth in the province of Galilee, had been born in Bethlehem. So he set out with Mary. She probably rode upon a donkey for she was expecting a Child. They arrived in Bethlehem after sunset and they went to an inn to ask for a room. The innkeeper came to the window and told them, "There's no room. All the inns are full. On your way now!"

74

So Joseph and Mary had to find room in a stall with the animals. While they were there, Mary said, "Joseph, I think that the Baby is coming." A little later, some shepherds who were watching over their flocks saw a great light approaching them. From that light an Angel told them, "Do not be afraid! I bring you good news that will fill every-one with joy. Today the Savior of the world is born in Bethlehem. He is wrapped in swaddling clothes and lying in a manger."

The shepherds rushed to Bethlehem. They found a Baby as the Angel had said. His parents were alongside Him, as were the animals who kept the Baby warm with their breath. They heard beautiful music coming from the heavens.

Wise Men Visit Jesus

SOME time later, three Magi, wise men, came from the East and presented themselves to King Herod in Jerusalem. They said, "Can you tell us where the King of the Jews has been born? We were guided here by a star, and we have come to pay Him homage." Herod was shocked and troubled by this. He considered himself to be the king of the Jews.

He immediately summoned the priests and his counselors who told him that this wondrous Child was born in Bethlehem. Herod summoned the Magi and told them, "The One Whom you are seeking is in Bethlehem. If you find Him, return here and tell me where He is so that I can go and pay homage to Him as well." What he was really planning to do, though, was to kill the Child. The Magi went their way, following

76

the star. They found the stall where the Child had been born. They knelt down and gave Him gifts, paying homage to the Baby Jesus.

After this, the Magi got ready to return to their homeland. That night they had a dream, and an Angel of the Lord told them, "Do not go through Jerusalem on your way back. Take a different route."

77

Flight into Egypt

JOSEPH also had a dream in which an Angel told him, "Joseph, take Mary and the Baby and flee to Egypt. Stay there until I tell you to return." Joseph immediately set off with Mary and the Child, riding on a donkey, and they crossed the desert to take refuge in Egypt. And it was just in time.

Herod, realizing that the Magi were not going to return to him, was enraged. He was both jealous and afraid of the Baby in Bethlehem Who would one day be the King of the Jews. Would the Child overthrow him and steal his crown? So Herod came up with a monstrous plan: he ordered that all boys in the area around Bethlehem who were two years old and younger be killed. Herod's soldiers rushed to that city and tore the babies from the mothers' arms. Without pity they killed them all, one by one. There was so much innocent blood, so many mothers' tears.

But Jesus had escaped the massacre of the Holy Innocents. He was safe in Egypt, where Mary and Joseph cared for Him. Jesus spent the next few years as a refugee, far from His homeland. One day, though, an Angel appeared to Joseph in a dream and told him, "Joseph, the danger is over. You can return to Israel with your wife and Child. Go to the city of Nazareth and take up your normal work." So Jesus grew up in Nazareth where He helped Joseph in his work as a carpenter and Mary in her housework.

Jesus in the Temple

SOME years later, when Jesus was twelve years old, He went with Joseph and Mary on their annual trip to Jerusalem for the feast of Passover. They traveled together with many of the other families of Nazareth. When they arrived, they went to the temple, the most important center of the Jewish faith. After that, they remained in Jerusalem for several days, praying and celebrating the Passover.

When it was time to go back home, they joined a caravan heading in that direction. After they had traveled some way, Mary found Joseph and asked him, "Where is Jesus? I can't find Him." Joseph answered, "Don't worry. He is probably playing with some of the other boys in the caravan." But Mary was still worried, so she began to search for Him.

As she passed from group to group of children, she grew more and more concerned because she did not find Him among them. Finally, panic stricken, Joseph and Mary left the caravan and returned to Jerusalem to search for Jesus. They said, "How could such a good Boy get lost? Could something bad have happened to Him?"

When they reached Jerusalem, they looked everywhere and asked everyone if they had seen Him, but everyone answered, "No, we haven't seen the Child you are describing." The poor parents looked around all that day, and then the next day as well, going from one neighborhood to the next, from one street to the next. They went on looking for Jesus the third day as well, growing more and more anxious as time went by. But still they could not find Him.

They asked themselves, "Has He disappeared, or did someone kidnap Him? Did He join another caravan, or maybe get lost in the desert where He might starve or die of thirst?" They had traveled all over Jerusalem. There was only one place where they had not yet been: the temple. But why bother going to the temple when there were only priests and wise men there? Could Jesus be there too? The two desperate parents decided to go there anyway and take a look.

That is exactly where they found Jesus. He was sitting there, speaking with the priests and wise men, asking them questions, just as if He were one of them. They were stunned. They asked themselves, "How could a Child Who was so young be so wise?" Mary asked Jesus, "My Son, how could You have let us worry so much?" Jesus answered, "Did you not know that I had to be about My Father's business?" Mary and Joseph did not understand as they looked at one another in confusion.

Jesus Is Baptized

A NUMBER of years later, when Jesus had grown up, He went down to the Jordan River to a man named John the Baptist. John was preaching the Word of God all throughout the land, baptizing people in the river.

Jesus humbly said to him, "Baptize Me, John the Baptist." But John, who immediately understood that Jesus was the Savior of the world, answered Him saying, "I should be baptized by You and not You by me." But Jesus said, "We must all do what we must do." So John the Baptist entered the Jordan River with Jesus and baptized Him. As he was pouring water over Jesus' head, there was a light in the heavens and a voice called out, "This is My chosen Son."

As soon as He was baptized, Jesus went off into the desert to meditate and pray to God His Father. The devil, who had followed Him into the desert, saw that Jesus was hungry and thirsty. He said to Him, "If You are the Son of God, turn these stones into bread." Jesus answered him, "Man does not live by bread alone, but by every word that comes from the mouth of God."

The devil then brought Him to the top of a mountain. Pointing to all the land that lay below, he said, "If You kneel down before me and worship me, I will give You all of the kingdoms on the earth." Jesus answered, "One must worship God alone."

82

Still, the devil did not give up. He carried Jesus in a whirlwind to the walls of the temple in Jerusalem. He said, "If You are the Son of God, throw Yourself down. We will see if Angels come to save You." Jesus answered, "You shall not tempt the Lord, your God." At that, the devil fled.

Call of the Apostles

ONE day Jesus was walking on the shores of the Sea of Galilee (which is also called the Sea of Tiberias). There He met some fishermen standing alongside of their boats. Jesus walked up to two of them, Simon and his brother Andrew, and He said to them, "Come, follow Me, and I will make you fishers of men." The two of them did not understand Him, but Jesus' goodness and holiness were so great that they immediately left their boats and followed Him.

A little later, Jesus approached two other brother fishermen, James and John, and He said the same thing to them. They too immediately followed Him. Some others followed Him as well, like Philip, because no one could resist Him.

Jesus traveled throughout Galilee with those first disciples, teaching them, preaching the Word of God, and healing many who were ill, paralyzed, lame, and despairing.

Wedding Feast at Cana

THERE was a wedding feast in the city of Cana to which Mary, Jesus, and His disciples had been invited.

There were many people there. At a certain point, the servants announced that they had run out of wine, which embarrassed the host. So Mary went over to her Son and said, "Do You know that they have run out of wine?" Jesus answered, "What business is that of ours, Mother? My time has not yet come." But Mary smiled and gave Him the look that meant that He should do something.

She then said to the servants, "Do whatever my Son tells you to do." Jesus saw some empty vases, and He ordered, "Fill these with water." When they had done what He had told them to do, He said to them, "Place them on the tables." When they were filling the first glasses, they noticed that red wine came out from the vases. It was so good that everyone was going over to the host and telling him how good it was. This was Jesus' first miracle.

Great Catch of Fish

JESUS returned to the shores of the Sea of Galilee and from His followers He chose Twelve Apostles. (This word, "Apostles," means messengers.) Among them were Simon, James, the son of Alphaeus, Simon the Zealot, and Judas Iscariot. Many were following Jesus, so He got into a boat in order to speak to them all. The crowd cried out, "You are the Son of God," but Jesus would not have it, for His time had not yet come.

The next morning, there was no one there. When Jesus woke up, He saw a boat, the one belonging to Simon. He had been fishing all night long, but had not caught anything. Jesus got into the boat and said, "Simon, throw your nets into the water one more time." Simon

When the boat finally reached the shore, Simon knelt down before Jesus. Realizing how he had doubted Him, he said, "Lord, leave me, for I am a sinner."

objected, "Lord, we have been fishing all night long, and we haven't caught even a single fish. But if You want me to, I'll throw the nets in one more time." He did this, not because he believed that it would work, but because Jesus had told him to do it. When he pulled up the nets, they were filled with big, fat fish. There were so many of them that he had to ask for help because he couldn't pull up the nets by himself. The boat, full of fish, almost sank; no one had ever seen such a big catch of fish.

Jesus Cures

PEOPLE hated and were afraid of lepers, and this is why they were kept as far away as possible from other people. A poor leper dragged himself over to Jesus. Jesus, unlike the others, did not run away from him. He stood still, awaiting him. The leper threw himself at His feet and said, "Lord, if You wish, You can heal me." Jesus reached out His hand and touched him saying, "I do wish it, be healed." All of the wounds that had been caused by the leprosy disappeared.

The leper who had been healed cried out for joy, and he wanted to show everyone that he had been cured of his leprosy. Jesus, however, said, "No! Do not tell anyone! Go to the priests and offer a sacrifice to God."

The leper made this promise to Jesus, but he couldn't keep his word. He cried out, "Look at me! It's me. Don't you recognize me? I'm healed!" Awestruck, they asked him, "Who healed you?" The healed leper answered, "Jesus, it was Jesus, the Son of God!"

He then joyously ran to show himself to everyone whom he could. Jesus became quite famous because of this. Many people came out to see Him and to listen to His preaching. Many of these were poor or they were ill and wanted to be healed. The wise men, priests, and doctors of the law also came out to see Him. Jesus went from district to district, from city to city.

One day He came to Capernaum. He arrived with a large crowd of His followers. He went into one of His friends' houses. There were so many people gathered around the house that no one could get in or leave through the door. Among the people in the crowd were four men who were carrying a stretcher that held a paralyzed man.

They cried out, "Make way! Make way! Let us through, we've got to go in to see Jesus!" But the crowd was too dense and they couldn't get through. They climbed up to the roof of the house and they moved some of the tiles aside, making

an opening. They then let down the stretcher with ropes. Jesus was moved with compassion. These men truly had faith in Him. He looked down at the paralyzed man who was looking up at Him with eyes filled with hope. He said to him, "My son, your sins are forgiven you."

Among those in the house were some priests who were scandalized by what He had said. They said to one another,

"Did you hear what He said? Blasphemy! Only God can forgive sins!" As soon as they had said this, Jesus, Who had overheard them, turned to them and said, "Which is easier to say, that your sins are forgiven or that you are to get up, take your stretcher and walk?" Then He said to the paralyzed man, "Get up, take your stretcher and go on your way!" The paralytic got up, took his stretcher and left, praising God the whole way out.

Sermon on the Mount

THE crowd that followed Jesus kept getting bigger and bigger. So Jesus climbed up a mountain and said:

"Blessed are the poor in spirit, for theirs is the kingdom of heaven.

"Blessed are those who mourn, for they will be comforted.

"Blessed are the meek, for they will inherit the earth.

"Blessed are those who hunger and thirst for justice, for they will be satisfied.

"Blessed are the merciful, for they will obtain mercy.

"Blessed are the pure in heart, for they will see God.

"Blessed are the peacemakers, for they will be called children of God.

"Blessed are those who are persecuted because they fight for justice, for theirs is the kingdom of heaven.

"Blessed are you when they hate you and persecute you, and when they tell all kinds of lies about you because of Me. Rejoice and be glad, for your reward will be great in heaven. This is how they persecuted the prophets who came before you.

"You are the salt of the earth. But if you become flat, what can restore your taste? You would be worth nothing more than to be tossed out into the street and trampled upon.

"You are the light of the world. A city set upon a hill cannot remain hidden. When you light a lamp, you do not hide it. You set it in a place where it can light up the whole house. That is how your light should shine before all. Your good works should be plain for all to see so that they can give glory to your Father Who is in heaven."

The people gathered on the mountain were still, listening as Jesus continued to speak.

He said, "Do not believe that I have come to abolish the law or the words of the prophets. I have not come to abolish them, I have come to fulfill them. In truth, I tell you, the heavens and the earth will pass away before a word or even a letter of the law will pass away.

"You have heard of old, 'An eye for an eye and a tooth for a tooth.' But I tell you, do not repay those who have harmed you. If they strike you on the right cheek, give them your other cheek as well. If they bring you into court to take your tunic, give them your cloak as well. If they make you walk one mile, walk two. Give to those who ask things of you, and do not reject those who seek a loan from you.

"You have heard, 'Love your neighbor and hate your enemy.' I tell you, love your enemy and speak well of those who mistreat you. If you love those who love you, what reward is there in that?

"Be perfect, as your Father in heaven is perfect. When you pray, pray like this: Our Father in heaven, holy is Your name. Your kingdom come, Your will be done, on earth as it is in heaven. Give us our daily bread, and forgive us our debts as we forgive our debtors. Do not lead us into temptation, but deliver us from evil. Amen."

Jesus Cures the Servant

ON their way back to Capernaum, Jesus met a Roman centurion. He was fit and strong with the proud air of a soldier. "Lord," said the centurion, "my favorite servant is lying paralyzed at home and he is suffering terribly." Jesus told him, "I will come to heal him." The eyes of the proud soldier filled with tears as he said, "Lord, I am not worthy for You to come into my house. Only say the word, and my servant will be healed. When I say to someone, 'Go,' he goes; to another, 'Do this,' he does it."

When Jesus heard this, He was profoundly impressed and turning to His disciples He said, "Truly, I have not found such great faith in all of Israel." Turning back to the centurion, He said, "Go, it will be as you have believed." The centurion returned home and his servant, who had been healed, was there waiting for him.

Widow of Naim

SOME time later, Jesus and His disciples were approaching the city of Naim. As He was about to enter the city gate, He saw a large crowd coming out. They were following a stretcher, weeping in silence. Upon the stretcher was the body of the only son of a poor widow, wrapped in a linen funeral shroud. His mother, who was now all alone in the world, was desperately weeping. Jesus was deeply moved when He saw her. He drew near and said, "Do not cry!"

The men who were carrying the body stopped where they were. Jesus approached the stretcher, put His hand on it, and said, "My son, I tell you, arise!" These simple words had a great effect, for the dead young man opened his eyes, began to breathe, sat up, and began to speak. He said, "I am alive! I am alive!" Jesus turned to the widow who was looking on astonished and said to her, "Mother, here is your son. I am giving him back to you."

He then went on His way, followed by His Apostles. The people who saw this miracle were astonished and they began to praise God. They knelt down and prayed, saying, "There is a great Prophet in our midst. God has visited His people."

Jesus Calms the Sea

SOME time later, Jesus and His disciples got into a boat to cross the lake. He was tired, and as He sat in the bow of the boat, He fell asleep. For a while nothing happened as the boat swept along on the calm water.

Suddenly, though, the wind came up and quickly grew more forceful. The sky darkened and the waves became more menacing. They loudly hit against the boat, spraying water into it. It seemed as if it were about to sink. The disciples struggled against the gusts of wind, trying to keep their boat on track.

Finally, having lost all hope, they woke up Jesus. They cried out, "Lord, save us!" Jesus looked up and asked them, "Why are you afraid? Don't you trust Me?" Getting up, He extended His arm and said, "Winds, be still! Waters, be calm!" The winds immediately grew still and the lake grew calm. The disciples fearfully asked, "Who is this that the winds and the waters obey Him?"

94

Jesus Casts Out a Demon

WHEN they reached the other shore, Jesus set off in the direction of the Gerasenes. There was a stillness in the air. All of a sudden they heard a scream, and a man who was possessed rushed out. He was clothed in animal skins, and he lived among the tombs. He would often assault people and they were all afraid of him. They even tried to bind him with chains, but he was so strong that he broke them and ran away.

The possessed man uttered some strange sounds and threw himself down at the feet of Jesus. Jesus said to the devil who possessed the man, "Come out, you unclean spirit!" The devil answered, "Don't send us away from here, Jesus." Jesus asked, "What is your name?" The demon answered, "My name is Legion. There are many of us in here. If You are going to cast us out, send us into the bodies of those pigs down there." Jesus said, "Let it be so." Instantly, the demons left the man.

He got up calm, as if he had been reborn. The herd of pigs, possessed by the demons, screamed out, ground their teeth and rushed off, falling into the lake where they disappeared. Jesus said to the man who had been healed, "Go home, and tell everyone what the Lord has done, how He had mercy on you."

Jairus's Daughter

JESUS returned to Capernaum. He was walking along, surrounded by a large crowd of people, when He met Jairus, an important official of the synagogue. Jairus knelt down in front of Jesus. He said, "Lord, my daughter is dying. Come give her a blessing and heal her." So Jesus followed Jairus, but the crowd became even more dense.

In the crowd there was a poor woman who had been ill for twelve years, suffering from a loss of blood, and no doctor was able to heal her. She thought, "If I could only touch Jesus, I would be healed." Motivated by her faith and her will to live, she pushed forward, reached out her hand, and touched Jesus. As soon as she touched Him, she was healed. Jesus, though, realized that someone had touched Him to be healed, and He had felt the power coming out from Him. He

stopped and stood still. He looked around and said, "Who touched Me?"

His disciples were confused and said, "Lord, with all of these people pushing in on us and reaching out to touch You, how can You ask, 'Who touched Me?'" Jesus repeated, "Who touched Me?" and continued to look around. The woman who had been healed came forward, trembling. She fell at His feet and said, "I touched You, Lord, because I wanted to be healed." Jesus gently asked her to get on her feet and He said, "Don't worry, My daughter. Your faith has saved you. Go in peace and be well."

He was still speaking when one of Jairus's servants arrived weeping and said, "It's too late, Jairus, your daughter died a few minutes ago." The crowd fell silent, and Jairus, pale and despairing, turned toward Jesus, but he couldn't even say a thing. Jesus tenderly told him, "Do not be afraid. Have faith in Me." He raised His arm and ordered no one to follow Him except for Jairus and a few of His disciples. He then went on His way.

When they arrived at Jairus's home, they heard the sound of weeping coming from inside. Jairus went in and saw his relatives and some other officials from the synagogue in mourning. Jesus said, "Why are you carrying on like this? Why are you crying so much? Get up! The child is not dead, she is only asleep."

Jesus firmly ordered everyone to leave the house. He then went into the room where the girl was laid out, taking with Him Simon Peter, James, John, and Jairus and his wife. Her face was as white as wax, and her eyes were closed. How could anyone not realize that she was dead? Jesus, though, calmly took her by the hand and said, "Little girl, I order you, get up!" As soon as He had said this, the little girl woke up as if she were getting up from a deep sleep and she rose to her feet. Frozen with fear, everybody looked on in silence. Jesus said, "Give her something to eat. But don't say anything to anyone."

97

John the Baptist Dies

KING Herod, the son of that horrible King Herod who had killed the Holy Innocents, arrested John the Baptist and threw him into prison. John was the man who had proclaimed the coming of the Messiah and had baptized Jesus in the Jordan.

This Herod was in love with the beautiful Herodias, the wife of his brother Philip. More than once John the Baptist had condemned him for this. Herodias, who was also in love with Herod, hated John the Baptist. She was the one who had convinced Herod to throw John the Baptist into prison and to put him to death. But Herod had not killed John the Baptist because he knew that John was a man of God. So he kept him locked up in his prison.

One day, Herod held a banquet. Herodias's beautiful daughter, Salome, began to dance. She danced so well that when she had finished, Herod said to her, "Salome, ask for anything you want and I will give it to you, even if you ask for half of my kingdom." The young girl ran to her mother and asked her, "Mother, what should I ask from the king?" The evil Herodias immediately said, "Ask him to give you the head of John the Baptist upon a platter."

Salome, as wicked as she was beautiful, returned to King Herod and said, "O king, I want you to give me the head of John the Baptist on a platter." King Herod was shocked by this request. He was a cruel man, but he was afraid to kill a prophet like John.

98

It must be John the Baptist, the one I killed. He has risen from the dead!" As his punishment, Herod was filled with guilt and fear every day for the rest of his life.

But he had made a promise loudly enough for everyone to hear. How could he now take it back? He was more afraid of looking bad in front of his guests than of committing a crime. So he sent an executioner to the prison to kill John. A short time later, a servant walked in carrying the head of John the Baptist on a platter and handed it to Salome who then brought it to Herodias.

When Herod heard that there was another Prophet in Galilee, called Jesus, Who was preaching the Word of God and performing miracles, he began to tremble and said, "No, it is not Jesus.

Jesus Feeds the People

though, word spread where He was, and a large crowd of people gathered on the lakeshore where they asked Him to teach them. Jesus preached and performed miracles because He had compassion on them. When the day drew on, Jesus' disciples said, "Master, it is late now, and this is a very deserted spot. Let the people go into the nearby villages to find something to eat."

Jesus smiled and told them, "There is no need to send them on their way to get something to eat. You can feed them." The disciples, confused, said, "Lord, we don't have enough food. In fact, the only food any of these people has is five loaves of bread and two fish, carried by a young boy. What could we do with so little food? How could we feed them all?"

SADDENED by the death of John the Baptist, Jesus and His disciples withdrew to an isolated place where they meditated and prayed to God. Soon,

100

Jesus said, "Bring Me those five pieces of bread and those two fish." They did this, and the boy came forward. Meanwhile, the people sat down; there were about five thousand of them, not counting the women and the children.

Jesus took the basket containing the bread and the fish, looked up into the heavens, and said to the Apostles, "Give these people something to eat." The Apostles, mystified, obeyed Him and began to hand out the bread and the fish. The basket seemed to have no bottom. The Apostles kept handing out the bread and the fish to the people who were pressing in on them, and there was enough for everyone.

So many hands were reaching out to them, and none of them was left empty.

Filled with awe, the disciples passed from group to group, giving everyone something to eat, praising the Lord the whole time. Everyone ate the bread and fish that had miraculously been multiplied until everyone was full.

The Apostles came back to Jesus and said, "Lord, we even have food left over from what You gave us." Jesus commanded them, "Gather up what is left over so that nothing goes to waste." The disciples obeyed and filled up twelve baskets with the leftover food. The people cried out, "Jesus is truly a Prophet. Let us make Him the King of the Jews." Jesus said nothing. He went off to a mountain all alone where He prayed and meditated.

Jesus Walks on Water

COMING down the mountain, Jesus said to His disciples, "Get in the boat and go to the other side of the lake, to the city of Bethsaida. I will tell the crowd to return to their homes." The disciples obeyed Him. Meanwhile, Jesus addressed the crowd and preached the Word of God to them again. He then told them to return to their homes. When He was alone again, He went back up the mountain to pray.

That evening, when it was late and getting dark, the wind began to blow and the waves grew high. The Apostles were in the middle of the lake in their boat. At first they were not afraid for some of them were fishermen who did not fear a sudden storm. But the darkness fell; the wind grew still stronger and the waves higher and higher. Soon they had to take down their sails because they were about to rip apart. They struggled to keep the boat on course.

One of the Apostles cried out, "What are we going to do?" One of the others said, "Who knows if we will reach the shore? Maybe we will all drown. I wish that the Master were with us now. He's not a sailor or a fisherman, but He could save us." They had just said these desperate words when one of them cried out, "Over there! Look over there!"

They all turned and saw a lone figure slowly walking toward them on top of the violent waves. The Apostles cried out, "It's a ghost! It's a ghost!" The Apostles were terrified as they gazed upon the vision and they clung to one another. Even though it was really only a matter of minutes, it seemed longer because of their fear. They then heard a familiar voice, "Do not be afraid. Be brave. It is I." The Apostles stammered, "It is the Lord! It is the Lord!" Simon cried out, "Lord, if it is You, command me to come to You across the waters." Jesus said to him, "Come here."

Simon got out of the boat and he slowly began to walk across the waves. Soon, however, he became afraid because of the roar of the wind. He began to hesitate. One foot slipped below the waters, even though it had held him up until then. Then the other foot began to sink as well. Simon Peter cried out, "Lord, I am sinking! Help me!" Jesus stretched out His hand and held him up, setting him up on his feet again. He said to him, "O man of little faith, why did you doubt?"

Without saying anything else, He came alongside the boat, still walking on the water. As soon as He got in the boat, the wind suddenly fell silent and the waves grew still. The lake was as calm as it had been before. The disciples in the boat fell on their knees and said, "You are truly the Son of God!" They raised their sails again and crossed the lake, joyfully coming to the other shore.

They got out of their boat in the territory of Gennesaret and word soon got around that Jesus was there. Everyone came running because they wanted to hear Him. Those who were suffering sought relief, and the ill and lame sought to be healed. Everyone who touched the hem of His garments was made well.

Jesus then went from that territory to the region around Tyre and Sidon, preaching and teaching. Crossing through the territory of Magadan, He arrived in an area called Caesarea. He remained there for several days.

The Transfiguration

ANOTHER time Jesus, along with Simon Peter, James, and his brother John, went up a desolate mountain. While they were praying, something wonderfully mysterious happened. Jesus was transfigured. His face began to shine as brightly as the sun. His dusty clothes became whiter than any bleach could make them. Two prophets appeared alongside of Him, Elijah and Moses, and they began to speak with Him.

Simon got up the courage to step forward and say, "Lord, it is good for us to be here. If You wish, Lord, John, James and I will pitch three tents, one for You, one for Moses, and one for Elijah."

Simon was still speaking when a gleaming cloud came down from the heavens and surrounded Jesus and the prophets. From the cloud came a thundering voice: "This is My beloved Son in Whom I am well pleased. Listen to Him." Upon hearing the voice, the disciples fell to the earth, trembling with fear. Jesus drew near them and said, "Get up! Do not be afraid!" The three Apostles obeyed and saw that Jesus was there alone. He was not gleaming anymore.

Going down into the valley, Jesus said to them, "Don't tell anyone what you have seen until the Son of Man will have risen from the dead." The disciples knew that when Jesus used the phrase, "the Son of Man," He was talking about Himself. But the disciples could not understand what He had meant when He said, "risen from the dead."

For a while they walked along, but eventually one of them asked Him, "Lord, the doctors of the law who know well the Sacred Scriptures say that Elijah must come first. What does that mean?" Jesus answered, "Elijah must come to set all things in order. But I tell you that Elijah has already come, yet people did not accept him. They treated him poorly. They will do the same to the Son of Man." The disciples understood that Jesus was not speaking about Elijah but of John the Baptist, who had come to announce the coming of the Messiah. They were saddened that Jesus was predicting that He would end up like John the Baptist: imprisoned and put to death.

Jesus Raises Lazarus

COMING down from the mountain, Jesus and the Apostles reunited with the other disciples. Not long thereafter, a friend of Jesus, a certain Lazarus, became ill. This Lazarus lived with his two sisters, Mary and Martha, in Bethany. The illness was very serious, and the two sisters sent word to Jesus, "Lord, the one whom You love is ill." Jesus commented, "His illness is not unto death, but so that the glory of God may be seen. Because of this, the Son of God will be glorified."

Instead of traveling to Bethany, He remained a couple of days with His disciples along the Jordan. He then said, "Let us go to Bethany. Our friend Lazarus has fallen asleep; let us go to wake him." The disciples said, "Master, if he is sleeping, he will get well." Jesus said, "Lazarus is dead, and I am happy for you that I was not there when he died so that you might believe. Come, let us go."

When they reached Bethany, Lazarus had already been in the tomb for four days. Martha came out to meet Jesus, weeping bitterly. She said to Him, "O Lord, if You had been here, my brother would not have died." Jesus, deeply moved, said, "Your brother will rise again." She said, "I know that, Lord. He will rise with everyone else on the last day." Jesus said, "I am the resurrection and the life. Whoever believes in Me, even if he should die, will live. Let us go to the tomb." Everyone followed Him there.

When they arrived, He stopped in front of the large stone rolled in front of the tomb. He said, "Roll back the stone." But Martha exclaimed, "But Lord, the smell will be awful. Lazarus has been dead for four days already."

Jesus answered, "If you believe, you will see the glory of God." They rolled back the stone, and after praying, Jesus cried out, "Lazarus, come out!" There was a profound silence as Lazarus came out of the tomb, still covered with his burial clothes. Jesus said, "Untie him, and let him go free!"

Jesus Calls Peter

MANY people began to believe in Jesus because of this miracle. In the meantime, Jesus went into the region around Caesarea with His disciples. One day He asked His companions, "What are people saying about Me?" They answered, "Some of the people say that You are John the Baptist, others Elijah or one of the prophets."

"And you," said Jesus, "Who do you believe Me to be?"

Peter answered, "You are the Christ, the Son of God." Jesus exclaimed, "Blessed are you, Simon, son of Jonah, because this is from God. From now on you will be called Peter, and on this rock I will build My Church, and the power of Satan will not destroy it." Jesus continued, "Peter, I will give you the keys of the kingdom of heaven. Everything that you will bind upon the earth will be bound in heaven. Whatever you loose on the earth will be loosed in the heavens." He then told the disciples not to tell anyone that He was the Christ, the Son of God.

Later on, some people brought children for Jesus to bless. Being young children, they were running around, laughing, playing, talking loudly. The one thing that they were not doing was standing quietly in line. This bothered the Apostles, and they grabbed hold of them, trying to make them stand around quietly. The children, however, raced ahead of them and reached Jesus first.

When the Apostles saw this, they lost their patience. Jesus, however, cried out, "No! Let the children come to Me! Do not hinder them! The kingdom of heaven belongs to such as these." The children then silently approached Him. Jesus continued, "I tell you, if someone is not as innocent as these children, that person cannot enter the kingdom of heaven." Having said this, Jesus embraced the children and blessed them.

The Prodigal Son

ONCE in a while, Jesus taught the crowds with parables. These were short stories that even the simple people could understand. Once He said, "A rich man had two sons. One day the younger son said to his father, 'Father, give me the part of the inheritance that belongs to me because I want to be on my way.' So the father divided his property in two portions. The younger son took his money and traveled to a distant land. There he enjoyed life. The other son stayed at home and kept working.

"The younger son squandered his wealth and ended up without any money. He was forced to care for pigs and feed them, and he was so hungry that he even had to eat the pigs' food. He thought to himself, 'My father's servants are better off than I am. I think I will go back to my father and tell him, "Father, I am sorry. I have sinned against heaven and against you. Don't treat me like a son anymore, treat me like a servant, but please let me come back."' Crying, he returned home to his father to say these things to him.

"Upon catching sight of him, his father embraced him and ordered that a great banquet be prepared. As the banquet was being held, the other son came in from the fields. When he saw what was happening, he said, 'What is this all about? Father, I always obeyed you, and you never gave me anything. And yet my brother returns, the same one who brought you nothing but grief and who wasted your money, and you throw a party for him?' The father answered, 'Son, you were always with me. Everything I had was yours. But we had to celebrate your brother's return. He was dead, and now he has returned to life. He was lost, and now he is found. So come celebrate with us.' "

Many people came to listen to Jesus proclaim His parables, even priests and doctors of the law. These said, "Look at this. He welcomes everyone and eats with them; He is even friendly to sinners."

Therefore, I assure you, there will be more joy in heaven for a repentant sinner than for the ninety-nine good people who had no need of repentance."

Then He added, "Behold, a woman had ten coins and lost one. Would she not search for it all throughout the house? And when she had found it, would she not say to her friends, 'I have good news. I found the coin that I lost!' Would she not say this? I tell you again, the Angels of God will rejoice more for one sinner who converts than for ninety-nine just people who did not need to convert."

The common thread of these parables is simple: those who walk in God's ways make God very happy, but God is even happier when someone who has lost his way returns to the right path.

When Jesus heard this, He said, "Who among you, when he has one hundred sheep and loses one, would not leave the ninety-nine to go search for the one that is lost? Who among you would not search for it until he had found it? When he found it, would he not place it on his shoulders and return home to say to his friends, 'Rejoice with me, my friends, because I have found my lost sheep!'

111

Workers in the Vineyard

JESUS then proclaimed another parable: "A man went out early in the morning to look for people to harvest the grapes in his vineyard. He went to the town square to look for those who were unemployed. He said to them, 'Go and work in my vineyard. I will pay you a just wage.' They agreed and went to work.

"A few hours later he passed by again and spoke to other unemployed people. He said, 'Go to my vineyard, and I will pay you a just wage.' Later on, he returned and went up to some unemployed people. He said to them, 'Why are you not working?' They said, 'Because no one has hired us.' 'Very well,' the man said, 'go into my vineyard and I will pay you a just wage.' And so they went.

"The day went by, and when the evening arrived, the workers brought their baskets filled with grapes to the man who had hired them. He paid them all the same wage. Those who had been the first to go to work in the vineyard said, 'How can this be? We've been working all day long, and you are paying us the same wage as you paid those who went to work later. Is that just?' The man answered, 'Friends, didn't we agree to this? Didn't I pay you a just wage? Take your money and go on your way. Or are you angry because I was so generous? Can I not do what I want with my own money?' "

Jesus concluded His parable by saying, "Remember that the last will be first and the first will be last. Many are called; few are chosen. This is how it will be in the kingdom of heaven."

112

The Good Samaritan

ONE of the doctors of the law came up to Him and said, "Master, what must I do to have everlasting life?" Jesus answered, "You must love God with your whole soul. You must love your neighbor as yourself." Another asked, "Who is my neighbor?" Jesus answered with another parable.

He said, "A man went along on the road that goes from Jerusalem to Jericho. Some robbers beat him up, robbed him and left him for dead. In a little while a priest came passing by. He saw the injured man, but he pretended not to and he went on his way. Then a Levite passed by, one who worked in the temple and should have had compassion on someone who was suffering. He too pretended not to see him and went on his way.

"Finally, a Samaritan passed by. He was not a Jew. In fact, Samaritans were enemies of the Jews, and the injured man was a Jew. The Samaritan saw him, stopped, and knelt down to help the poor man. He put medicine on his wounds and lifted him on his donkey. He carried him to the nearest inn where he could recover. He had to move on because he had some urgent matters to take care of. He gave the innkeeper some money and asked him to take care of the injured man. He told him, 'If you spend more on him, I will repay you on my return trip.' "

So Jesus said to the doctor of the law, "Well, according to you, who was the neighbor of the injured man: the priest, the Levite, or the Samaritan?" He answered, "It was the Samaritan who showed him the most mercy." Jesus answered, "Good; then go and do the same."

Zacchaeus

JESUS was about to enter the city of Jericho and many came out to see Him. A certain Zacchaeus went to see Him as well. He was not liked because he was a tax collector. He climbed a tree to get a better look at Jesus. Jesus saw him and said, "Climb down from there, Zacchaeus. Today I am going to stay at your home." Zacchaeus climbed down from the tree and welcomed Jesus into his home. But the people mumbled, "Look at that. Jesus is eating with a dog like him." When Zacchaeus heard what they were saying, he said, "Master, I will give half of my money to the poor, and if I have cheated anyone, I will pay them back four times over." Affectionately, Jesus said, "O Zacchaeus, today salvation has visited your home."

Jesus Enters Jerusalem

JESUS was now approaching Jeru-salem. He arrived at the city of Bethany and said, "Go, find a young donkey that is tied up. Untie it and bring it to Me. If anyone asks you, 'What are you doing?' tell that person that you are doing it for Me, and they won't bother you." The disciples obeyed Him. Finding the young donkey, they untied it. Its owner came upon them and said, "What are you doing?" The disciples answered, "We are doing it in Jesus' name."

The Apostles brought the donkey to Jesus, and He rode it into Jerusalem. A large crowd of people greeted Him. Many honored Him by laying down their clothes in the street for Him to walk upon so that He would not get dirty. Others cut off branches from the trees and spread them on the ground, crying out, "Blessed is He Who comes in the name of the Lord. Peace on earth and glory in the heavens!"

The priests in the temple and the doctors of the law were upset by all this. They complained, "Everyone is going out to meet Him. We cannot do anything to Him."

The Last Supper

THE Feast of Passover was coming, and Jesus knew that the time for Him to leave this world was approaching. It was sad, for He loved life, but He also knew that He had come down to earth to die as a sacrifice for us all. The evening that they sacrificed the lamb for Passover, Jesus sat down with His Twelve Apostles to eat His Last Supper with them.

He poured out water from a container to wash the feet of the Apostles, and He dried them with a towel He had tied around His waist. When it was Peter's turn, Peter said to Him, "Are You, Lord, going to wash my feet?" Jesus said to him, "What I am doing, Peter, you do not now understand, but one day you will understand." Peter answered, "Lord, You cannot wash my feet." Jesus told him, "If I can't wash them, Peter, you will have no part with Me." Peter, deeply moved, said, "O Lord, then wash not only my feet, but my head as well." Jesus said, "If someone is clean, he only needs to have his feet washed. You are clean, although not all of you." He said this because He knew that one of His disciples was about to betray Him. There was a profound silence.

When Jesus sat down again at table with His disciples, He continued the meal and said, "Truly, I tell you, one of you will betray Me." Disturbed and saddened, each of the Apostles asked, "Lord, am I the one who will betray You?" When Judas Iscariot asked, "Lord, am I the one who will betray You?" Jesus looked at him and said, "You have said so." They continued to eat their meal, but they lost their appetite and were sad.

Later, Jesus took a piece of bread, broke it, gave it to the disciples, and said, "Take and eat this, all of you. This is My body." After they had eaten it, He took a cup filled with wine and said, "Take this and drink it, all of you, because this is My blood, a sign of the new covenant between God and man. It will be poured out for many for the forgiveness of sins. Whenever you do this, do it in memory of Me." Thus Jesus gave us the Eucharist. Then, Judas Iscariot excused himself and went on his way. He went to tell the priests that it was almost time to arrest Jesus.

Jesus and the others got up to pray, and He said to them, "You will all be shaken tonight. But it is written, 'I will strike the shepherd and the sheep will be scattered.'" He was telling them that He was the Shepherd

and that He would be taken away from them, and that the Apostles, the sheep, would be scattered. He continued, "But when I will be raised, I will go before you into Galilee." Peter said, "Lord, I will never be shaken. Even if everyone else is disturbed by what happens, I will not be disturbed."

Jesus gently told him, "O Peter, truly I tell you, tonight before the rooster crows, you will deny Me three times." Shaking his head, Peter exclaimed, "No, Lord! I will never deny You, even if I had to die with You." All the other disciples expressed similar thoughts as Peter did. Jesus said, "Believe in God and believe in Me. There is much to do in My Father's house, and I am going to prepare a place for you. When it is prepared, I will return to take you away. You know where I am going; you know the way." The disciple Thomas said, "Lord, we do not know where You are going. How can we know the way?" Jesus said to him, "I am the way, the truth, and the life."

Agony in the Garden

JESUS went with His disciples to a hill called Gethsemane. He took Peter, James, and John with Him, and He left them near the entrance to pray. He became very sad and said to them, "My soul is sorry unto death. Stay here and stay awake with Me."

He then went on a little and He began to pray saying, "Father, take this cup away from Me. Yet not My will, but Your will be done." He returned to the disciples and found them sleeping. He said to Peter who woke up confused, "Peter, are you sleeping? Can you not stay awake with Me for a single hour? Now stay awake and pray not to fall into temptation, for the spirit is willing but the flesh is weak." Then He went off again to pray.

Returning to them two more times, He found them sleeping again. The third time He said, "Get up; let's go!

The time has come for the Son of Man to be handed over to sinners. The one who is going to betray Me is near."

118

Judas Betrays Jesus

SOON they heard the sound of an approaching crowd. Holding torches, swords, and lances, men climbed up the hill of Gethsemane to arrest Jesus. Among them was the traitor Judas Iscariot who had said to the others, "Be on your guard. You are to arrest the Man Whom I kiss." He came up through the crowd and drew near Jesus Who was standing with the Apostles. He said, "Greetings, Master," and he kissed Him. Jesus said, "Judas, would you betray Me with a kiss?"

The mob came forward for that had been their signal. Jesus asked them, "Whom are you looking for?" They answered, "Jesus of Nazareth!" He said, "I am He." At these words, they all fell to the ground. He asked again, "Whom are you looking for?" They said, "Jesus of Nazareth!" Jesus replied, "I told you that I am He." Looking at the Apostles who were also surrounded, He said, "If you want Me, then let them go."

Peter took out a sword and cut off the ear of one of the priest's slaves. Jesus scolded him, though, saying, "Enough! Put back your sword, Peter! He who lives by the sword will die by the sword." Turning to the people He said, "Why have you come after Me with swords and clubs, as if I were a thief? Why did you not arrest Me in the temple when I was there with you? But this is the way it must be so that My fate might be fulfilled." They crowded around Him, put Him in chains, and led Him away. The disciples, confused and frightened, fled.

Jesus before Caiphas

JESUS was dragged before the council of the priests. They were looking for an excuse to put Him to death. Two false witnesses lied saying, "This Man said, 'I can destroy the temple in Jerusalem and rebuild it in three days.'" The high priest Caiphas got up and exclaimed, "This is blasphemy. Come forward, Jesus. How do You answer this charge?" But Jesus remained silent.

Caiphas then said, "Tell me if You are the Christ, the Son of God." Jesus answered, "You have said so. In a little while you will see the Son of Man seated at the right of God Almighty." When he heard this, Caiphas tore at his clothes, thus showing how scandalized he was. He cried out, "He has blasphemed. You all have heard it. We do not need any more witnesses. What do you say?" Everyone present yelled out, "He is guilty! He is guilty! He deserves to be put to death. Yes! Yes! He must be put to death! Kill Him! Kill Him!" Those who were most agitated surrounded Jesus Whose hands were bound. They screamed at Him, cruelly pushing and insulting Him. The meanest of them began to slap Him, saying, "You know everything, Christ! Who slapped You?"

Peter Denies Jesus

MEANWHILE Peter (who, from a distance, followed the mob that had dragged his Master away) entered the courtyard of the building where they were meeting. He took his place among others, warming himself at a fire. He stood there in silence, waiting for some news.

All of a sudden, a woman looked over at him and said, "Aren't you one of Jesus' disciples?" Everyone angrily glared at Peter, but he forced a smile and said, "Who me? I don't even know whom you are talking about." Then, pretending that nothing was wrong, he went out from the courtyard. As he was leaving, another woman came up to him and cried out, "You! You were with Jesus!" "Me? No," answered a very disturbed Peter, "I swear it's not true!"

But the people surrounded him. One raised a torch to shine on his face. Someone else said, "Yes! Yes! You are one of Jesus' disciples. Admit it. You are a disciple of Jesus." Peter then yelled back, "Me, a disciple of Jesus? I don't even know Who He is. I don't know Him. I've never seen Him before!" At that very instant, they heard a rooster crow. Peter fell silent, remembering what Jesus had said, "Before the rooster crows, you will deny Me three times." Weeping and despairing, he ran away.

"You have said it." Pilate continued, "Did you not hear all they are accusing you of?" But Jesus did not answer him. Pilate did not find anything wrong in what Jesus had done, but nevertheless he handed Him over to the priests who took Jesus to Herod. This Herod was the son of Herod the Great, the king who had killed the Holy Innocents.

He interrogated Him, but Jesus would not say a word to him. They then brought Jesus back to Pontius Pilate, who then handed Him over to the Roman soldiers. These soldiers were cruel men who couldn't care less Who He was. They chained Him to a column and stripped Him. They then savagely lashed Jesus with whips. Yet, He did not cry out as they beat Him mercilessly.

Others arrived and began to mock and beat Him terribly, saying, "You claim that You are the King of the Jews. Really? What a fool!" Another soldier hissed, "You're a King, but You don't even have a robe." And he thrust an old, moth-eaten red robe upon His bloody shoulders. More soldiers gathered around Jesus, spit in His face, and insulted Him. One cried out, "Now You have a robe, but You don't have a crown

Jesus Is Scourged

BY this time it was morning, and they brought Jesus before Pontius Pilate, the Roman governor. The Romans were in charge of Israel, and the Jews could not do anything without their permission. The priests said to Pontius Pilate, "This Man wanted to incite the people to rebellion. He told them that they did not have to pay the taxes that you Romans impose, and He said that He was the King of the Jews." The priests were sure that these charges were serious enough to convince Pilate to put Jesus to death.

Pontius Pilate asked Jesus, "Are You the King of the Jews?" He answered,

122

yet." Another said, "I'll take care of that." He went out and found some twigs filled with thorns and he wove them into a type of crown. He then cruelly pounded it down upon Jesus' head. The thorns cut into Jesus' flesh and the blood began to pour down upon His face. Still, Jesus did not cry out; He did not even say a word. He stood there, pale, but solemn.

Pontius Pilate was looking at what was happening from a window. He still thought that Jesus was innocent. He believed that Jesus was an honest and just man. Could he let Him go free? No! The priests and Herod, who were important people, would be against it. Should he condemn Him? But for what? Pontius Pilate thought to himself, "Maybe this crowd that the priests have gathered will feel sorry for Jesus when they see what a bloody mess He is. Maybe they will let me release Him."

123

Jesus Is Condemned

PILATE went to his balcony. The crowd under him had been quite loud, but when they saw him they quieted. Pilate cried out, "I am going to bring out Jesus now. I don't find any fault in Him." Jesus was brought out, covered in the red cloak and with the crown of thorns on His head. Pilate showed Him to the crowd and said, "Behold the Man!" He was hoping that the crowd would feel sorry for Jesus, but the priests and the guards began to cry out, "Crucify Him! Crucify Him!"

So Pilate looked for another way to save Jesus. He cried out, "Since it is a feast, I want to free a prisoner who has been condemned to death. There are two of them: Jesus and the murderer Barabbas. Tell me, whom do you want me to free, Jesus or Barabbas?" Incited by the priests, they shouted out, "Barabbas! Barabbas! Free Barabbas!" Pilate then asked, "What should I do with Jesus?" "Crucify Him! Crucify Him!"

Fearful, the Roman governor went back into the palace and had Jesus brought before him. He asked Him, "Where do You come from?" Since he got no answer, he said, "Are You not going to talk to me? Don't You know that I have the power to crucify You or to let You go free?" Jesus answered, "You would have no power if it were not given to you from above. Because of this, the one who handed me over is more guilty than you."

Yet, Pilate still looked for some way to set Jesus free. At this, the priests said, "Be careful! If you don't condemn Jesus, it means that you are not a friend of the emperor!" So he gave up and handed over Jesus to be crucified. They put a heavy wooden beam on His shoulders that He was forced to carry. They led Him along to the hill called Golgotha (or Calvary), where those condemned to death were executed.

Jesus Carries His Cross

JESUS, bearing the weight of that beam, stumbled along the streets of Jerusalem. As He went along, the soldiers and the servants of the priests forced Simon, a resident of Cyrene, to help Him. There were also a number of weeping women along the way. Jesus fell down more than once because He was so weak, but the punches and kicks of the soldiers forced Him to get back up again and continue on His way.

There were two other condemned prisoners with Him who were to be crucified. They were thieves. When they were later lifted up on their crosses, they acted in different ways. One blasphemed and shouted out to Jesus, "If You are the Son of God, save us and Yourself." The other thief said, "Don't tell me that, even though you're a thief like me, you have no fear of God even now. We deserve to die; we are only being condemned for our crimes, but Jesus did not do anything wrong."

Turning to Jesus, Who was crucified between the two, he said, "Lord, remember me when You come into Your kingdom." Jesus looked at him and said, "Truly, today you will be with Me in Paradise."

Jesus Is Crucified

WHEN Jesus arrived at Calvary, the place where He would fulfill His destiny, they removed His cloak and threw Him down to the ground. They stretched out His arms on the beam of the Cross. They then nailed Him to the Cross. While they were doing this, Jesus looked to the heavens and said, "Father, forgive them. They don't know what they are doing." A Roman official stood nearby with a sign upon which was written, "Jesus of Nazareth, King of the Jews." The soldiers stripped Jesus, and they cast dice to see who would get His cloak.

When they had nailed Jesus to the beam, they raised Him up on the Cross. Someone in the crowd cried out, "You saved others, but You can't save Yourself!" But there were also some standing nearby who loved Him: Mary, His mother; her sister Mary, the wife of Cleophas; Mary Magdalene; and the young Apostle John.

126

Jesus Dies

THE sky grew darker, and Jesus cried out from the Cross, "My God, My God, why have You abandoned Me?" And then He died. The earth shook and the people felt their hearts tremble. The Son of God was dead.

Burial of Jesus

WHEN Jesus was dead, the crowd there fled because they were frightened by the darkness that had covered the heavens. Even as they fled, some said, "Truly, this was the Son of God." The women and the disciples took down the body of Jesus from the Cross and, weeping, placed it on the earth. Jesus' mother Mary took Him in her arms and mourned her Son's death.

There was a rich and well-respected man among those who believed in Jesus

130

whose name was Joseph of Arimathea. He showed himself to be courageous as well when he came before Pontius Pilate and said, "I have come here to ask for the body of Jesus of Nazareth Who died upon the Cross." Pilate had not yet heard that Jesus was dead. He asked a centurion if it were true. He answered, "Yes, He is dead. To be sure that He was dead, one of the soldiers had gone over to the Cross and wounded Him in His side with a lance, and blood and water came out." Pontius Pilate said, "Joseph of Arimathea, your wish is granted. I give you permission to take the body of Jesus."

The good man Joseph was comforted by this, and he went to buy a new piece of linen with which he could wrap the body. The pious women who had remained to weep under the Cross helped him prepare the body of Jesus for burial. Nicodemus also came forward to help them. He was a pious man of faith, and he brought an ointment made from myrrh and aloes, two fragrant and precious perfumes.

The body of Jesus was washed, anointed, wrapped in linen, and placed in the tomb. This was the tomb that Joseph of Arimathea had prepared for himself. It had been dug out from the rock on a hillside on his property. This tomb had never been used. So Joseph of Arimathea carried Jesus' body there. They had a large rock rolled over the opening to the tomb. The rock was so large that it would take several men to roll it away. Having completed this holy work, the pious women, Joseph of Arimathea, and Nicodemus left in silence to weep and pray.

body and then say, 'See, Jesus is not in the tomb anymore. He must have risen. He must truly be the Son of God.' In order to prevent this, order that your soldiers keep guard over the tomb for three days." So Pontius Pilate ordered Roman soldiers be sent to watch over the tomb where Jesus had been buried.

The priests said, "Very good! This way Jesus' disciples can't trick anyone. If they convince the people that their Master has risen, then this new fraud would be worse than anything Jesus had done up to now." The Roman soldiers, guided by the priests, went to guard the tomb.

Jesus died on the evening before the Sabbath. On the third day after His death, Mary Magdalene and some other pious women went to the tomb, bringing

Jesus' Resurrection

THE chief priests came to Pilate and told him, "Lord, you know that Jesus Whom you justly crucified once said, 'I will rise from the dead after three days.' His disciples could rob the ointment to anoint the body of Jesus. As they walked along, they said to each other, "Who will move for us that huge rock that is covering the tomb?" But when they drew near, they saw that the large rock that had covered the entrance to the tomb had been rolled back. The guards were lying on the ground, confused and a little afraid.

When they went into the tomb, they saw two Angels who said to them, "Whom are you looking for?" The women answered, "We are looking for Jesus, our Lord." The Angels answered, "Why are you looking for the living among the dead? He is not here. He has been raised."

The pious women, deeply moved and frightened, ran on their way, looking for the eleven Apostles. They told them and the other disciples what they had seen and heard. But the Apostles did not believe the women. They thought that the women's grief had caused them to see things. Nevertheless, Peter went to the tomb. The only thing he saw was the linen cloth lying on the ground. He was deeply moved, but could not yet believe that Jesus was truly risen.

He went back to the others and said, "Something strange has happened. The tomb is empty. Our Master's body is gone." One of the disciples asked, "What are we going to do?" He answered, "I don't know. Let's go somewhere and wait, away from those who put Jesus to death. What else can we do?" But they still did not understand what had happened.

Road to Emmaus

THAT same evening, two disciples were heading toward Emmaus, a village not too far from Jerusalem. They were walking along, discussing what had happened. While they were talking, Jesus approached them and began to walk along with them, although they did not recognize Him.

As they walked along, He asked them, "Why are you so sad?" One of them answered, "Don't you know what happened in Jerusalem? You must be a stranger here." Jesus asked, "What happened?" So they told him about the arrest, condemnation, and death of their Master. They said, "We had hoped that He was the Savior of Israel, but that doesn't seem to be the case. Now three days have gone by. Some of our women have confused us because early this morning they went to the tomb and found it empty. They ran to tell us that they saw some Angels who told them that Jesus is risen. Even Peter went to the tomb, but he did not find Him."

Jesus said to them, "Oh foolish men, how can you not believe? Didn't Christ say that He had to suffer first and then enter into His glory?" He then began to explain to the two what was written about Him in the Sacred Scriptures. When they had arrived in Emmaus, Jesus pretended to want to continue on His way. The two disciples said, "Stay with us because it is getting late. The day is almost over." They all went to an inn and sat down for supper.

Jesus took a piece of bread in His hands and broke it, just as He had done at the Last Supper. He gave it to the disciples. At that instant, the disciples' eyes were opened and they realized He was Jesus. Just as quickly, Jesus disappeared from their sight. The two of them said, "It is He. Didn't our hearts burn within us as we heard Him speak about the Sacred Scriptures?" They immediately turned back and ran to the eleven and the other disciples with them, and said, "Our Lord is truly risen."

Jesus Appears to the Apostles

ONE of the Apostles, Thomas, did not believe that Jesus had risen. He wanted to touch the nail marks in His hands and place his finger in the wound in His side." Some days later, the disciples were gathered in a locked room because of their fear.

Jesus came into the room, although He had not opened either the doors or the windows. He said to them, "Peace be with you." To Thomas He said, "Place your finger here, look at My wounds, and stop doubting. Believe!" Falling on his knees, Thomas exclaimed, "My Lord and my God." Jesus said, "You have believed because you have seen. Blessed are those who have not seen but believe."

Another time Jesus appeared to His disciples on the shore of Lake Tiberias. The Apostles were fishing, and they saw their Master standing on the shore. Peter jumped into the water to swim to Jesus. Jesus asked him three times, "Peter, do you love Me?" Three times Peter answered, "Lord, You know that I love You." Jesus told him, "Tend My sheep." To the Apostles Jesus said, "Go throughout the whole world and preach the Good News. Baptize those who believe so that they might be saved. Those who refuse to believe will be condemned." Then Jesus ascended into the heavens.

135

Spreading the Gospel

THEY went all throughout the world, preaching the Good News, the words of Jesus. This was the Apostles' mission. Many of those who heard it became Christians, followers of Jesus Christ. This is how the first Christian communities were founded. Men and women lived together in harmony, praying, and breaking bread just as Jesus had commanded them to do, in faith and love. Every day the Lord sent new Christians to live with them, adding to the number of those who believed in the true God and in the eternal life that He offered them.

Stoning of Stephen

AMONG the most famous Christians was a man named Stephen, who was filled with grace and preached in a way that was truly inspired by God.

He brought many people to conversion and performed many miracles. Some of the priests, who were enemies of anyone who followed Jesus, sought him out and had him falsely accused of blasphemy. Stephen was brought before the priests' court, but he defended himself so well, so sincerely, that his enemies, even though they were furious at him, could not convict him. Stephen finished his speech saying,

"Behold, I see the heavens opening and the Son of Man standing on the right hand of God." Jesus had said similar words when He stood before Caiphas. The reaction of the priests was the same. They tore at their clothes to show how scandalized they were.

Stephen was rushed outside of Jerusalem. As soon as he was outside of the city, the crowd began to throw stones at him. They attacked him savagely, knocking him to the ground. Their assault continued. At last, Stephen uttered, "Lord, forgive them their sin," and he died.

Conversion of Saul

AMONG those who persecuted the Christians, and who in fact had assisted those killing Stephen, was a man named Saul. He was so intent on persecuting Christians that he attacked them wherever he found them. Saul, a Roman citizen, even considered them to be enemies of Rome.

Once, he set out from Jerusalem with some soldiers to go to Damascus to arrest and try them. A brilliant light came down from the heavens and surrounded him. His horse was frightened by it and threw him off. Saul heard a loud voice from the heavens say, "Saul, Saul, why are you persecuting Me?" Shaking, Saul asked, "Who are You, Lord?" The voice from the heavens answered, "I am Jesus Whom you are persecuting." Saul, still trembling, said, "What do You want me to do, Lord?" He answered, "Get up, go into Damascus.

There I will make known to you what you are to do." Saul got up, but he could not see anything for he was blind. Those who were with him had to lead him into Damascus by hand. God had called him to be a Christian and to preach His Word throughout the whole world.

some of them, they mocked him; in some, they sent him away. In still others, they threatened him or laughed at him. But there were also those who listened to him and were moved by his words. Touched by God's grace, they began to believe in the Word of Jesus. It was as if Paul was scattering the seed; from then on, the plant of the Christian faith grew in Greece.

It was not only Paul who was traveling throughout the world preaching the Gospel. The Apostles did the same thing, even if the Acts of the Apostles speaks mostly about what Paul said and did. This was so that those who did not know Jesus would see how people were ready to embrace the Faith and preach it.

Paul: "Lion of God"

IN Damascus, Saul came to know some other Christians, and through them the Apostles. He soon came to be known as Paul, the Roman form of his name. The Apostles welcomed him as one of their own because they realized that God's grace had poured down upon him. Paul was eventually to be known as the "Lion of God," because he began to proclaim the Word of Jesus throughout the whole world.

He even preached in the capital of Greece, Athens, a beautiful city filled with culture and wealth. There were many well-educated people there, and not just the shepherds and fishermen found in Israel. Many Greeks made fun of Paul, but he did not let this discourage him. He continued to preach fearlessly. He traveled from city to city. In

139

Deaths of Peter and Paul

PAUL preached about Christ in Rome as well. Peter, the Apostle whom Jesus had placed in charge of His whole Church, also reached the capital of the world. It was in Rome, in the year 65 A.D., that the emperor Nero began a persecution against Christians. He wanted to blame them for the fire that had destroyed much of the city July 18 and 19 in 64 A.D. Peter was crucified, but he humbly said that he was not worthy to be crucified the same way that Jesus was. He asked to be crucified upside down. He died calling upon the name of his Lord.

Paul, who had been thrown in prison again, was put on trial and convicted. He was not crucified. He had his head cut off at a site called the "Three Fountains," about three miles outside the city of Rome. He wrote in one of his letters, "I have fought the good fight. I have kept the faith. Now, a crown of justice awaits me, which the Lord will give me as my reward. But it will not only be given to me. It will be given to all those who longingly await His glorious return. The Lord, our God, will bring me home to His heavenly kingdom. To Him be glory forever."

OTHER OUTSTANDING CATHOLIC BOOKS
FOR CHILDREN

FIRST BOOK OF SAINTS—By Rev. Lawrence G. Lovasik, S.V.D. A magnificent full-color book about the Saints, featuring a full-page illustration of each Saint. **No. 133**

PICTURE BOOK OF PRAYERS—Beautiful book of prayers for children featuring prayers for the day, major feasts, various occasions and special days: First Communion, Confirmation, Name Day and Birthday. **No. 265**

NEW CHILDREN'S MASS BOOK—This Mass Book contains the basic responses for every Holy Mass. Enables children to take a more active part in the Mass. Ideal for First Communicants and all young children. Easy to follow. **No. 807**

PICTURE BOOK OF SAINTS—By Rev. Lawence G. Lovasik, S.V.D. Illustrated lives of the Saints in full color for young and old. It clearly depicts the lives of over 100 popular Saints in word and picture. **No. 235**

ILLUSTRATED LIFE OF JESUS—By Rev. Lawrence G. Lovasik, S.V.D. A large-format book with magnificent full-color pictures for young readers to enjoy and learn about the life of Jesus. With simple, easy-to-read language, this timeless book about the greatest life ever lived will be treasured by all who use it. **No. 935**

MY GUARDIAN ANGEL—By Rev. Thomas J. Donaghy. Inspiring book about Guardian Angels that will teach children about Angels and the part they play in our lives. 16 beautiful illustrations in full color. **No. 125**

BOOK OF PRAYERS FOR CHILDREN—A beautifully illustrated book that introduces children to prayer. Prayers for each day, prayers to the Trinity, to the Saints and Angels, and for Family and Friends. **No. 148**

THE MASS FOR CHILDREN—By Rev. Jude Winkler, OFM Conv. Beautifully illustrated Mass Book that explains the Mass to children and contains the Mass responses they should know. It is sure to help children know and love the Mass. **No. 215**

WHEREVER CATHOLIC BOOKS ARE SOLD